Web Riches: The Roadmap to Online Earnings

Avinash Walton

Published by Avinash Walton, 2023.

While every precaution has been taken in the preparation of this book, the publisher assumes no responsibility for errors or omissions, or for damages resulting from the use of the information contained herein.

WEB RICHES: THE ROADMAP TO ONLINE EARNINGS

First edition. August 13, 2023.

ISBN: 979-8224878765

Written by Avinash Walton.

Table of Contents

INTRODUCTION

Welcome to "Web Riches: The Roadmap to Online Earnings" – your ultimate guide to unlocking the potential of the internet to earn money and build a thriving online business. In this book, I, Avinash Walton, will take you on a journey through various online income opportunities, providing you with the strategies and insights you need to harness the power of the digital revolution. Whether you're a seasoned entrepreneur or just starting your online journey, this book will help you navigate the vast landscape of online earning possibilities, avoid common pitfalls, and pave your way to financial success. Get ready to embark on a rewarding adventure where the internet becomes your gateway to wealth and prosperity.

<u>DISCLAIMER</u>

The information provided in this book, "Web Riches: The Roadmap to Online Earnings," is intended for educational and informational purposes only. The author, Avinash Walton, and the publisher are not responsible for any actions taken by individuals based on the content of this book. The success and results achieved in earning money online may vary based on individual skills, dedication, and market conditions. Readers are advised to conduct their own research and exercise due diligence before making any financial decisions.

Ch 1. Understanding the Online Landscape

The internet has revolutionized the way we live, work, and connect with others. In this chapter, we will delve into the online landscape and gain a deeper understanding of its impact on traditional job markets, the advantages and challenges it presents, and how to identify your skills and strengths for online ventures.

1.1 The Digital Revolution and its Impact

THE DIGITAL REVOLUTION refers to the transformative impact of technology, particularly the internet, on various aspects of our lives. This section will explore the profound effects of the digital revolution on traditional job markets and industries, as well as the opportunities it has created for online earning.

1.1.1 Transformation of Traditional Job Markets:

SHIFT FROM TRADITIONAL brick-and-mortar businesses to online platforms: With the rise of e-commerce, many businesses have transitioned to online platforms, leading to a decrease in the demand for physical storefronts and an increase in remote work opportunities.

Disruption of traditional industries: The digital revolution has disrupted industries such as publishing, music, and retail, challenging established business models and creating new avenues for online earning.

Job automation and artificial intelligence: Automation has impacted certain job sectors, with tasks being performed by machines and algorithms. However, it has also given rise to new roles and opportunities in emerging fields related to AI and machine learning.

1.1.2 Remote Work and Freelancing:

REMOTE WORK OPPORTUNITIES: The internet has enabled individuals to work remotely, breaking geographical barriers and allowing for flexibility in where and how work is conducted. This has become especially prevalent in knowledge-based professions such as programming, writing, design, and customer service.

Freelancing platforms and marketplaces: Online platforms like Upwork, Freelancer, and Fiverr have facilitated the connection between freelancers and clients, allowing individuals to offer their skills and services on a project basis.

1.1.3 Democratization of Information and Knowledge:

ACCESS TO INFORMATION: The internet has made information readily accessible to people worldwide, levelling the playing field for those seeking knowledge and learning opportunities.

Online education and e-learning: Platforms like Coursera, Udemy, and Khan Academy offer online courses and educational resources, allowing individuals to acquire new skills and qualifications from the comfort of their homes. This has created new opportunities for both learners and educators alike.

1.1.4 Entrepreneurship and Startups:

LOWER BARRIERS TO ENTRY: The internet has significantly reduced the costs associated with starting a business. Online platforms and tools enable aspiring entrepreneurs to create and launch their products or services with minimal upfront investment.

Global reach and customer base: Online businesses can reach a global audience, allowing entrepreneurs to tap into larger markets and customer segments beyond their local communities.

Disruptive innovations and market niches: The digital revolution has given rise to disruptive innovations and the identification of untapped market niches. Entrepreneurs can leverage these opportunities to create unique online businesses and revenue streams.

1.1.5 Digital Economy and New Job Opportunities:

EMERGENCE OF DIGITAL roles: The digital revolution has brought forth new job roles and opportunities, such as digital marketing specialists, social media managers, data analysts, and user experience designers.

Gig economy platforms: Platforms like Uber, Airbnb, and TaskRabbit have created opportunities for individuals to offer services on a freelance or part-time basis, contributing to the gig economy and providing additional avenues for online earning.

Conclusion:

THE DIGITAL REVOLUTION has had a profound impact on traditional job markets, creating both challenges and opportunities. It has transformed industries, facilitated remote work and freelancing, democratized access to information, fostered entrepreneurship, and given rise to new job opportunities in the digital economy. Understanding these changes and adapting to the online landscape is crucial for anyone seeking to earn money online. In the following chapters, we will explore various strategies and opportunities available for online earning.

1.2 Advantages of Earning Money Online

EARNING MONEY ONLINE offers numerous advantages over traditional forms of income generation. In this section, we will explore some of the key advantages that make online earning an attractive option for many individuals.

1.2.1 Flexibility and Work-Life Balance:

- **LOCATION INDEPENDENCE:** Online earning allows you to work from anywhere with an internet connection. Whether you prefer working from the comfort of your home, a coffee shop, or while traveling, the flexibility of online work enables you to design your own workspace.

- **Flexible schedules:** Unlike traditional 9-to-5 jobs, online earning often allows for flexible working hours. You can choose when to work based on your preferences and personal commitments, providing greater control over your time and allowing for better work-life balance.

- **Multiple income streams:** Online earning often provides the opportunity to diversify your income sources. You can explore different online ventures simultaneously, such as freelancing, affiliate marketing, or e-commerce, allowing you to generate income from multiple channels.

1.2.2 Global Reach and Access to a Vast Customer Base:

- **EXPANDED MARKET OPPORTUNITIES:** The internet has made it possible to reach a global audience. Online businesses and entrepreneurs can tap into markets beyond their local communities, increasing their potential customer base and revenue streams.

- **Targeted marketing and personalization:** With online earning, you can leverage digital marketing strategies to reach specific target audiences. Online platforms offer tools and analytics that enable precise targeting and personalization, allowing you to tailor your products or services to meet the needs of your ideal customers.

1.2.3 Low Startup Costs and Overhead:

- **REDUCED INITIAL INVESTMENT:** Starting an online business or pursuing online earning opportunities often requires lower initial investment compared to traditional businesses. You can launch a website, create digital products, or join freelancing platforms with minimal upfront costs.

- **Lower operational expenses:** Online businesses typically have lower overhead costs compared to brick-and-mortar establishments. There's no need for physical storefronts, inventory storage, or extensive equipment. This cost advantage allows you to allocate more resources to marketing, product development, or scaling your online venture.

1.2.4 Access to Learning and Skill Development:

- **ABUNDANCE OF ONLINE resources:** The internet offers a wealth of educational content, tutorials, courses, and communities that can help you acquire new skills or enhance existing ones. Online earning provides an opportunity to continuously learn and adapt to emerging trends and technologies.

- **Rapid skill acquisition:** Online learning platforms often offer self-paced courses, allowing you to learn at your own convenience and progress at a speed that suits you. This flexibility enables you to acquire new skills efficiently and apply them directly to your online earning endeavors.

1.2.5 Entrepreneurial Opportunities:

- EMPOWERMENT AND INDEPENDENCE: Online earning allows individuals to become their own bosses and take control of their financial futures. It empowers you to turn your passions, skills, or expertise into profitable online businesses.

- Scalability and growth potential: Online ventures have the potential to scale rapidly, as the internet provides a platform for exponential growth. With effective marketing strategies, automation tools, and the ability to reach a global audience, online businesses can expand quickly and generate significant income.

1.2.6 Lower Environmental Impact:

- REDUCED CARBON FOOTPRINT: Working online eliminates the need for daily commuting, resulting in less traffic congestion and reduced carbon emissions. Online earning contributes to a greener environment by minimizing the environmental impact associated with transportation.

Conclusion:

EARNING MONEY ONLINE offers numerous advantages that make it an appealing choice for individuals seeking flexibility, global reach, low startup costs, access to learning, entrepreneurial opportunities, and a reduced environmental impact. By leveraging the power of the internet, you can create a sustainable source of income while enjoying the freedom to work on your own terms. In the next chapters, we will explore specific strategies and opportunities for earning money online.

1.3 Challenges of Earning Money Online

WHILE EARNING MONEY online offers numerous advantages, it also comes with its own set of challenges. In this section, we will explore some common challenges that individuals may face when pursuing online earning opportunities.

1.3.1 Increased Competition:

- **SATURATED MARKETS:** The online landscape is highly competitive, with many individuals and businesses vying for attention. Finding a niche or unique selling proposition becomes crucial to stand out among the competition.

- **Global competition:** With the internet's global reach, you are not only competing with individuals or businesses in your local area but also with professionals from around the world. This requires continuous improvement and adaptation to stay competitive.

1.3.2 Self-Motivation and Discipline:

- **LACK OF STRUCTURE:** Online earning often means working independently without direct supervision. This can lead to a lack of structure and discipline if you're not proactive in managing your time and setting goals.

- **Self-motivation:** Without the external pressure of a traditional workplace, it's important to stay motivated and focused on your online earning pursuits. Maintaining a strong work ethic and being accountable to yourself are essential.

1.3.3 Scams and Fraudulent Activities:

- **ONLINE SCAMS:** The internet is not without its share of scams and fraudulent schemes. It's crucial to be vigilant and cautious when exploring online earning opportunities. Research and verify the legitimacy of platforms, clients, or investment opportunities before committing your time or resources.

- **Protecting personal information:** Online earning involves sharing personal information and financial details. Safeguarding your data from potential breaches and identity theft is essential. Implementing security measures such as strong passwords and using trusted platforms with secure payment gateways can help protect your online presence.

1.3.4 Technological Advancements and Changing Trends:

- **RAPIDLY EVOLVING LANDSCAPE:** The online world is constantly evolving, with new technologies, platforms, and trends emerging regularly. Keeping up with these changes and adapting to new tools, algorithms, or marketing strategies can be challenging but crucial for sustained success.

- **Continuous learning:** To stay competitive, it's essential to engage in continuous learning and upskilling. The need to acquire new skills or update existing ones can be a challenge, especially for individuals with limited time or resources.

1.3.5 Online Reputation Management:

- **ONLINE REPUTATION:** Your online reputation plays a vital role in building trust with potential clients or customers. Managing your online presence, addressing customer feedback, and maintaining a positive brand image require effort and attentiveness.

- **Negative feedback and criticism:** Dealing with negative reviews or criticism online can be challenging. It's important to respond professionally, address concerns, and learn from constructive feedback to improve your online reputation.

1.3.6 Connectivity and Technical Issues:

- **RELIANCE ON INTERNET** connectivity: Online earning heavily relies on a stable internet connection. Technical issues or disruptions can hinder productivity and impact your ability to work effectively.

- **Troubleshooting technical problems:** Dealing with technical issues, software glitches, or website maintenance can be time-consuming and frustrating. Having basic technical knowledge and troubleshooting skills can help mitigate these challenges.

Conclusion:

WHILE EARNING MONEY online presents numerous advantages, it is important to recognize and navigate the challenges that come with it. Increased competition, self-motivation, scams, technological advancements, online reputation management, and connectivity issues are some of the common challenges individuals may face. By being aware of these challenges and developing strategies to overcome them, you can enhance your chances of success in the online earning landscape. In the upcoming chapters, we will explore specific strategies and opportunities that can help you navigate these challenges and build a successful online earning venture.

1.4 Identifying Your Skills and Interests

IDENTIFYING YOUR SKILLS and interests is a crucial step in the process of earning money online. Understanding your unique strengths and passions will help you align your online ventures with areas where you can excel and find fulfillment. In this section, we will explore how to assess your skills, interests, and marketable strengths for online earning.

1.4.1 Self-Assessment of Skills:

- **REFLECT ON YOUR PAST experiences:** Consider your previous work, educational background, and personal projects. Identify the skills you have acquired through these experiences, such as communication, problem-solving, writing, design, programming, or marketing.

- **Identify transferable skills:** Transferable skills are abilities that can be applied to various fields. These may include organizational skills, teamwork, leadership, time management, or adaptability. Assess which transferable skills you possess and how they can be leveraged in an online context.

- **Seek feedback:** Reach out to friends, colleagues, or mentors and ask for their input on your strengths and skills. Sometimes, others can offer valuable insights that you may not have considered.

1.4.2 Exploring Your Interests and Passions:

- **IDENTIFY YOUR HOBBIES and interests:** Consider the activities that bring you joy and fulfilment outside of work. Whether it's writing, photography, cooking, fitness, or gaming, your hobbies can provide clues about areas where you have a genuine passion and could potentially monetize online.

- **Analyse your favourite subjects or topics:** Think about the subjects or topics that captivate your interest. Whether it's technology, fashion, personal development, or finance, your passion for specific subjects can lead you to opportunities for creating content, offering expertise, or engaging in online communities.

- **Assess personal goals and values:** Consider your long-term goals and values. Aligning your online earning pursuits with your personal values can bring a sense of purpose and fulfilment to your work. For example, if you value environmental sustainability, you may explore online ventures related to eco-friendly products or services.

1.4.3 Identifying Marketable Strengths:

- **RESEARCH MARKET DEMAND:** Investigate the current trends and demands in the online marketplace. Identify areas where there is a growing need or a gap that you can fill with your skills and expertise.

- **Analyse competitors:** Study successful individuals or businesses in your desired niche. Understand what sets them apart and how you can differentiate yourself by leveraging your unique strengths.

- **Seek feedback from potential clients or customers:** Engage with your target audience to gather insights on their needs and pain points. This feedback can help you identify areas where your skills can provide solutions and value.

1.4.4 Bridging the Gap:

- **IDENTIFY AREAS FOR improvement:** Assess areas where you may need to develop or enhance your skills to align with online earning opportunities. Explore online courses, tutorials, or resources that can help you acquire the necessary knowledge and expertise.

- **Experiment and refine:** Start with small projects or experiments within your identified skills and interests. Continuously evaluate and refine your approach based on feedback and results. This iterative process will help you narrow down your focus and discover what works best for you.

Conclusion:

IDENTIFYING YOUR SKILLS and interests is a crucial step in the online earning journey. By understanding your unique strengths, passions, and marketable abilities, you can align your online ventures with areas that bring you fulfilment and have market demand. Regular self-assessment, exploring your interests, seeking feedback, and bridging any skill gaps will help you build a strong foundation for success in the online earning landscape. In the upcoming chapters, we will delve into specific online earning strategies and opportunities that align with your identified skills and interests.

1.5 Overcoming Myths and Misconceptions

WHEN IT COMES TO EARNING money online, there are numerous myths and misconceptions that can create unrealistic expectations or deter individuals from pursuing online earning opportunities. In this section, we will address some common myths and misconceptions and provide insights to help you navigate the online earning landscape effectively.

1.5.1 Myth: "Get Rich Quick" Schemes:

ONE PREVALENT MYTH is the promise of quick and easy wealth through online ventures. It's essential to understand that genuine online earning requires effort, dedication, and time to build sustainable income streams.

- **Reality:** Earning money online is like any other endeavour - it requires hard work, persistence, and a long-term mindset. Be wary of schemes or programs that promise overnight success with minimal effort. Instead, focus on developing valuable skills, providing quality products or services, and building a solid foundation for your online ventures.

1.5.2 Myth: Online Earning is for Tech Experts Only:

ANOTHER MISCONCEPTION is that online earning is limited to individuals with advanced technical skills or expertise.

- **Reality:** While technical skills can be advantageous in certain online ventures, there are numerous opportunities available for individuals with diverse skill sets. From freelance writing and graphic design to social media management and online tutoring, the online landscape offers a wide range of options that cater to various talents and interests. Focus on leveraging your existing skills and continuously learning new ones as needed.

1.5.3 Myth: Online Earning is Not Reliable or Secure:

SOME PEOPLE BELIEVE that online earning is inherently risky or insecure, associating it with scams or fraudulent activities.

- **Reality:** While there are risks involved in any online endeavour, there are also plenty of legitimate and secure opportunities available. Research and due diligence are crucial when selecting platforms, clients, or investment opportunities. Choose reputable platforms, implement security measures to protect your personal information, and stay vigilant to identify and avoid potential scams.

1.5.4 Myth: Online Earning is Isolated and Lacks Community:

ONE MISCONCEPTION IS that online earning means working in isolation without the support of a community or network.

- **Reality:** The online world is rich with communities, forums, and networking opportunities that can connect you with like-minded individuals and provide support. Joining industry-specific forums, online groups, or attending virtual conferences can help you expand your network, collaborate with others, and learn from their experiences.

1.5.5 Myth: Online Earning is Limited to a Few Industries:

SOME PEOPLE BELIEVE that online earning is limited to a specific set of industries, such as technology or creative fields.

- **Reality:** The online landscape offers diverse opportunities across various industries, including education, healthcare, e-commerce, consulting, marketing, and more. Identify your skills, interests, and market demand to explore the online earning potential within your chosen industry or niche.

1.5.6 Myth: Online Earning Requires Expensive Investments:

THERE IS A MISCONCEPTION that online earning requires significant upfront investments in technology or marketing.

- **Reality:** While there may be initial costs involved in setting up an online venture, such as creating a website or investing in equipment, many online earning opportunities have low entry barriers and can be started with minimal investment. You can leverage affordable or free online tools and platforms to launch and grow your online business gradually.

Conclusion:

OVERCOMING MYTHS AND misconceptions is crucial to approaching online earning with a realistic mindset. Understand that online earning requires effort, time, and continuous learning. Focus on developing your skills, identifying legitimate opportunities, and building a strong foundation for success. By dispelling myths and misconceptions, you can navigate the online earning landscape effectively and set yourself up for sustainable income generation. In the upcoming chapters, we will delve into specific strategies and opportunities for earning money online, providing you with practical guidance to achieve your goals.

1.6 Online Learning and Skill Development

IN THE DIGITAL AGE, online learning has become an invaluable resource for acquiring new skills and enhancing existing ones. This section explores the importance of online learning and skill development in the context of earning money online.

1.6.1 Abundance of Online Learning Resources:

- **LEARNING PLATFORMS:** There are numerous online platforms dedicated to education and skill development, such as Coursera, Udemy, LinkedIn Learning, and Khan Academy. These platforms offer a wide range of courses, tutorials, and resources covering various subjects and disciplines.

- **Massive Open Online Courses (MOOCs):** MOOCs provide access to high-quality courses from renowned universities and institutions around the world. They often offer flexibility in terms of schedule and pace of learning.

- **Specialized websites and blogs:** Many websites and blogs are dedicated to sharing knowledge and expertise in specific areas. These platforms offer articles, tutorials, and guides that can help you acquire specific skills related to your online earning pursuits.

1.6.2 Advantages of Online Learning:

- **FLEXIBILITY AND CONVENIENCE:** Online learning allows you to learn at your own pace and convenience, fitting it into your schedule. You can access courses and resources from anywhere with an internet connection, making it accessible to learners worldwide.

- **Diverse learning formats:** Online courses often offer a variety of learning formats, including video lectures, interactive quizzes, assignments, and discussion forums. This multimodal approach caters to different learning preferences and enhances engagement.

- **Cost-effective:** Online learning is often more affordable compared to traditional in-person education. Many courses and resources are available at lower costs or even for free, allowing you to acquire new skills without significant financial burden.

- **Lifelong learning:** Online learning encourages a culture of lifelong learning, where individuals can continuously acquire new skills and stay updated with the latest trends and technologies. This is particularly important in the dynamic online earning landscape, where adaptability and continuous improvement are essential.

1.6.3 Identifying Relevant Skills for Online Earning:

- **RESEARCH MARKET DEMAND:** Before selecting specific skills to develop, research market trends and demands within your chosen niche or industry. Identify the skills that are in demand and align with your online earning goals.

- **Consider transferable skills:** Transferable skills are versatile abilities that can be applied across different roles and industries. These include skills such as communication, problem-solving, critical thinking, time management, and collaboration. Assess your existing transferable skills and identify areas where you can further enhance them.

- **Assess emerging skills:** Keep an eye on emerging skills that are becoming increasingly relevant in the digital landscape. These may include skills related to artificial intelligence, data analysis, digital marketing, coding, user experience (UX) design, or virtual reality (VR).

1.6.4 Creating a Learning Plan:

- **SET SPECIFIC GOALS:** Define clear learning goals based on the skills you want to develop and the online earning opportunities you want to pursue. Set milestones and deadlines to track your progress.

- **Break it down:** Break down your learning goals into smaller, manageable steps. Identify the specific topics or sub-skills you need to focus on and create a learning roadmap accordingly.

- **Allocate time and resources:** Dedicate regular time to learning and skill development. Create a study schedule or allocate specific time slots for online learning activities. Identify the resources, courses, or tutorials that will help you achieve your learning goals and utilize them effectively.

- **Practice and apply knowledge:** Learning doesn't end with acquiring theoretical knowledge. Actively apply your skills through practical projects, freelance work, or personal initiatives. This hands-on experience will strengthen your skills and build a portfolio for future online earning opportunities.

Conclusion:

ONLINE LEARNING AND skill development are essential components of earning money online. By leveraging the abundance of online learning resources, you can acquire new skills, enhance existing ones, and stay ahead in the rapidly evolving digital landscape. Identify relevant skills, set learning goals, create a learning plan, and allocate dedicated time for skill development. Through continuous learning, practice, and application, you can enhance your capabilities and unlock new opportunities for online earning. In the following chapters, we will explore specific strategies and opportunities that you can pursue based on your acquired skills and knowledge.

1.7 Building a Strong Online Presence

IN THE DIGITAL AGE, building a strong online presence is essential for success in earning money online. An effective online presence helps you establish credibility, reach your target audience, and promote your products or services. This section explores strategies for building a strong online presence to enhance your online earning endeavors.

1.7.1 Create a Professional Website or Online Portfolio:

- **DOMAIN AND HOSTING:** Register a domain name that reflects your brand or professional identity. Choose a reliable hosting service to ensure your website is accessible and performs well.

- **Design and layout:** Create a visually appealing website or online portfolio that reflects your brand image. Ensure it has a user-friendly interface, easy navigation, and showcases your skills, work samples, or offerings effectively.

- **Content creation:** Regularly update your website or portfolio with fresh and engaging content. This can include blog posts, case studies, client testimonials, or project showcases. Quality content helps establish your expertise and provides value to your audience.

1.7.2 Optimize Your Social Media Profiles:

- **CONSISTENT BRANDING:** Maintain consistent branding across your social media profiles. Use the same profile picture, cover photo, and bio to reinforce your brand identity.

- **Engaging content:** Share valuable content, industry insights, or updates related to your online earning pursuits on social media. Interact with your audience by responding to comments, messages, and participating in relevant discussions.

- **Network and collaboration:** Engage with like-minded individuals, industry professionals, and potential clients or customers on social media platforms. Build relationships, collaborate on projects, and seek opportunities for growth.

1.7.3 Leverage Content Marketing:

- **BLOGGING:** Start a blog on your website or contribute guest posts to relevant publications. Share informative and engaging articles that demonstrate your knowledge, expertise, and insights in your niche. This helps attract organic traffic, establish authority, and engage with your target audience.

- **Video content:** Create video content on platforms like YouTube or LinkedIn. Share tutorials, educational content, or industry-related insights through videos. Visual content can be highly engaging and help you reach a wider audience.

- **Podcasting:** Consider starting a podcast to share your expertise, interview industry experts, or discuss relevant topics. Podcasting allows you to connect with your audience in an intimate and informative way.

1.7.4 Engage in Online Communities and Forums:

- **JOIN RELEVANT COMMUNITIES:** Identify online communities, forums, or social media groups related to your niche. Participate actively, contribute valuable insights, answer questions, and engage with other members. This helps you establish credibility and build relationships within your industry.

- **Provide value:** Offer help, share your knowledge, and provide valuable resources to the community. Be authentic and genuinely contribute to discussions. This positions you as an expert and builds trust with potential clients or customers.

1.7.5 Build a Personal Brand:

- **DEFINE YOUR BRAND identity:** Determine your unique selling proposition and what sets you apart from others in your industry. Develop a clear brand identity that reflects your values, expertise, and personality.

- **Consistent messaging:** Ensure consistency in your brand messaging across all online channels. Use a consistent tone, style, and language that resonates with your target audience.

- **Online reputation management:** Monitor and manage your online reputation by responding to feedback, reviews, or comments promptly and professionally. Establish a positive online reputation by providing excellent customer service and maintaining integrity in your online interactions.

1.7.6 Networking and Collaboration:

- **ATTEND VIRTUAL CONFERENCES and events:** Participate in virtual conferences, webinars, or industry events related to your online earning pursuits. Network with industry professionals, exchange ideas, and explore potential collaborations or partnerships.

- Seek guest posting opportunities: Contribute guest posts to reputable blogs or publications in your industry. This expands your reach, establishes your authority, and exposes you to new audiences.

Conclusion:

BUILDING A STRONG ONLINE presence is vital for success in earning money online. Create a professional website or online portfolio, optimize your social media profiles, leverage content marketing, engage in online communities, and build a personal brand. Networking, collaboration, and actively participating in industry-related activities further enhance your online presence. By implementing these strategies, you can establish credibility, reach your target audience, and promote your online earning ventures effectively. In the following chapters, we will delve into specific strategies and opportunities that align with your strong online presence.

1.8 Online Safety and Security

WHEN ENGAGING IN ONLINE earning activities, it's crucial to prioritize safety and security to protect your personal information, financial transactions, and online presence. This section explores important considerations and measures to ensure online safety and security.

1.8.1 Protecting Personal Information:

- STRONG PASSWORDS: Use unique, strong passwords for your online accounts. Include a combination of uppercase and lowercase letters, numbers, and special characters. Avoid using easily guessable information like your name or birthdate.

- **Two-factor authentication (2FA):** Enable 2FA whenever possible. This adds an extra layer of security by requiring a second verification step, such as a code sent to your mobile device, in addition to your password.

- **Privacy settings:** Regularly review and adjust privacy settings on your social media accounts, websites, or any other online platforms you use. Limit the amount of personal information visible to the public or adjust settings to restrict access to certain groups.

- *Avoid phishing attempts:* Be cautious of suspicious emails, messages, or websites that ask for personal information or credentials. Avoid clicking on suspicious links or downloading files from unknown sources.

1.8.2 Secure Online Transactions:

- **TRUSTED PAYMENT GATEWAYS:** When accepting payments or making purchases online, use trusted payment gateways that offer secure and encrypted transactions. Research and choose reputable payment processors to ensure the safety of financial information.

- **SSL certificates:** If you operate an online store or handle sensitive customer data, consider obtaining an SSL (Secure Sockets Layer) certificate. This encrypts data exchanged between your website and users, ensuring secure communication and protecting customer information.

1.8.3 Protecting Online Reputation:

- **ONLINE REPUTATION management:** Regularly monitor your online presence, including social media accounts, reviews, and comments about your online earning activities. Respond promptly and professionally to feedback or complaints, addressing any concerns and maintaining a positive reputation.

- **Professional communication:** Maintain professionalism in all your online interactions. Be mindful of the language, tone, and content you share on your website, social media, or other online channels. Use appropriate privacy settings to separate personal and professional communications.

1.8.4 Secure Website and Data Protection:

- **REGULAR SOFTWARE UPDATES:** Keep your website software, plugins, and scripts up to date to ensure you have the latest security patches. Regular updates help protect against vulnerabilities that could be exploited by hackers.

- **Backup data:** Regularly back up your website, database, and other critical data. Store backups in secure, offsite locations or use reliable cloud storage services to protect against data loss or potential security breaches.

- **Website security plugins:** Consider using security plugins or tools that provide additional layers of protection against common online threats, such as malware, hacking attempts, or brute-force attacks.

1.8.5 Educate Yourself on Online Threats:

- **STAY INFORMED:** Keep yourself updated about the latest online security threats, scams, and best practices. Follow reliable sources such as cybersecurity blogs, reputable news outlets, or industry-specific forums that provide insights and tips for staying safe online.

- **Cybersecurity awareness training:** Consider participating in cybersecurity awareness training courses or workshops. These resources can provide you with knowledge and skills to identify and mitigate online risks effectively.

Conclusion:

PRIORITIZING ONLINE safety and security is crucial when engaging in online earning activities. Protect your personal information, secure online transactions, and safeguard your online reputation. Keep your website and data secure through regular updates and backups. Educate yourself on online threats and stay vigilant to protect against potential risks. By implementing these measures, you can create a safe and secure online environment for your earning pursuits. In the following chapters, we will explore specific strategies and opportunities for earning money online while maintaining online safety and security.

CHAPTER CONCLUSION

UNDERSTANDING THE ONLINE landscape is the first step towards successfully earning money online. By recognizing the opportunities, advantages, and challenges presented by the digital revolution, you can better position yourself to capitalize on the vast potential of the internet. Identifying your skills and interests, overcoming myths and misconceptions, investing in learning, and establishing a strong online presence will set the foundation for your online earning journey. In the upcoming chapters, we will delve into specific strategies and opportunities that you can explore to start generating income online.

Ch 2. Freelancing and Remote Work

———

Freelancing and remote work have become increasingly popular in the online earning landscape. In this chapter, we will delve into the world of freelancing and remote work, exploring how to leverage your skills, find opportunities on freelance platforms, build a freelance portfolio and personal brand, negotiate rates and contracts, and effectively manage clients to deliver high-quality work.

2.1 Exploring Freelance Platforms and Marketplaces

FREELANCE PLATFORMS and marketplaces have revolutionized the way individuals find work and businesses hire talent. In this section, we will explore popular freelance platforms and marketplaces, and provide insights on how to navigate and leverage them to find online freelance opportunities.

2.1.1 Upwork:

UPWORK IS ONE OF THE largest freelance platforms, offering a wide range of job categories and projects. Here's how to get started on Upwork:

- **Creating an Upwork profile:** Sign up and create a detailed profile that highlights your skills, experience, and portfolio. Provide specific examples of your work and showcase your expertise.

- **Skill tests and certifications:** Take skill tests relevant to your area of expertise to demonstrate your proficiency. Earn certifications, such as Upwork's "Top Rated" or "Rising Talent" badges, to enhance your credibility.

- **Bidding on projects:** Browse available projects and submit proposals that showcase your understanding of the client's needs and how you can fulfill them. Craft compelling proposals that highlight your unique value proposition and address the client's requirements.

2.1.2 Freelancer:

FREELANCER IS ANOTHER popular freelance platform with a large user base. Here's how to explore opportunities on Freelancer:

- **Building your Freelancer profile:** Create a professional profile that highlights your skills, experience, and portfolio. Optimize your profile with relevant keywords to increase visibility in search results.

- **Bidding on projects:** Browse available projects and submit bids that outline your qualifications, proposed timeline, and pricing. Tailor your bids to each project and emphasize how you can add value to the client's project.

- **Showcasing your expertise:** Participate in Freelancer contests or skill tests to demonstrate your abilities and gain recognition. This can help attract potential clients and establish your expertise within the Freelancer community.

2.1.3 Fiverr:

FIVERR IS A FREELANCE platform known for its gig-based model, where freelancers offer services starting at $5. Here's how to make the most of Fiverr:

- **Creating a gig:** Define the services you offer and create compelling gig descriptions that clearly communicate the value you provide. Use eye-catching visuals and include relevant samples of your work to attract potential buyers.

- **Optimizing gig tags and keywords:** Research keywords and tags that are relevant to your services and optimize your gig for search results. This helps increase your visibility and attract the right clients.

- **Offering gig extras and packages:** Upsell additional services or create different packages to provide more options for clients. This allows you to offer a range of pricing options and cater to different client needs.

2.1.4 Guru:

GURU IS A PLATFORM that connects freelancers with businesses looking for specific skills and expertise. Here's how to navigate Guru effectively:

- **Building a professional profile:** Create a comprehensive profile that highlights your skills, experience, and portfolio. Showcase your expertise and provide relevant examples of your work to build trust with potential clients.

- **Showcasing your work:** Utilize Guru's workroom feature to collaborate with clients and showcase your work progress. This helps establish transparency and build client confidence in your abilities.

- **Leveraging the Workroom feature:** Use Guru's Workroom to manage projects, communicate with clients, and share files and deliverables. This centralized platform streamlines project management and facilitates efficient collaboration.

2.1.5 Other Platforms:

APART FROM THE AFOREMENTIONED platforms, there are several other freelance marketplaces and platforms you can explore, such as Toptal, 99designs, PeoplePerHour, and Gigster. Research and identify platforms that align with your skills and target clientele to broaden your freelance opportunities.

Conclusion:

EXPLORING FREELANCE platforms and marketplaces provides you with access to a wide range of online freelance opportunities. Whether you choose Upwork, Freelancer, Fiverr, Guru, or other platforms, it's important to create a compelling profile, showcase your expertise, and tailor your proposals or gigs to attract potential clients. By effectively leveraging freelance platforms and marketplaces, you can expand your online earning opportunities and find projects that align with your skills and interests.

2.2 Leveraging Your Skills to Find Remote Work Opportunities

REMOTE WORK OFFERS the flexibility to work from anywhere while leveraging your skills and expertise. In this section, we will explore strategies for identifying and pursuing remote work opportunities that align with your abilities and interests.

2.2.1 Identify Your Marketable Skills:

- **EVALUATE YOUR SKILLS:** Take an inventory of your skills and expertise. Consider both technical and soft skills that are relevant to remote work. This could include programming, graphic design, content writing, project management, customer service, or language proficiency.

- **Assess transferable skills:** Identify transferable skills that can be applied to remote work, such as communication, time management, adaptability, problem-solving, and teamwork. These skills are valuable in remote work settings where self-discipline and collaboration may be essential.

2.2.2 Research Remote Work Industries and Job Boards:

- **EXPLORE REMOTE-FRIENDLY** industries: Research industries that have a high demand for remote work. This could include areas like technology, digital marketing, writing and editing, virtual assistance, consulting, or online education. Look for industries that align with your skills and interests.

- **Utilize remote job boards:** Browse remote job boards and websites that specialize in remote work opportunities. Some popular remote job boards include Remote.co, We Work Remotely, Flex Jobs, and Remote OK. These platforms aggregate remote job listings across various industries and provide filters to narrow down your search.

2.2.3 Network and Leverage Online Platforms:

- **UTILIZE PROFESSIONAL** networking platforms: Leverage platforms like LinkedIn to connect with professionals in your field and explore remote work opportunities. Join relevant industry groups and participate in discussions to expand your network and gain insights.

- **Freelance platforms and marketplaces:** In addition to traditional job boards, consider registering on freelance platforms (such as Upwork, Freelancer, or Fiverr) to find remote freelance projects that align with your skills. These platforms allow you to showcase your expertise and connect with clients seeking remote talent.

2.2.4 Polish Your Online Presence:

- **OPTIMIZE YOUR ONLINE profiles:** Ensure your professional profiles, such as LinkedIn or freelance platform profiles, are complete and up to date. Highlight your remote work experience, skills, and accomplishments.

- **Develop a remote-focused resume:** Tailor your resume to highlight remote work skills, such as self-motivation, time management, and remote collaboration. Emphasize any relevant remote work experience or remote-friendly projects you have completed.

2.2.5 Showcase Your Remote Work Skills:

- **BUILD A REMOTE WORK portfolio:** Create a portfolio that showcases your remote work projects or examples of work relevant to the remote work industry you are targeting. Include case studies, samples, or links to remote work you have successfully completed.

- **Demonstrate remote work competencies:** Highlight your ability to work independently, manage projects remotely, and communicate effectively in virtual environments. Share specific examples of how you have utilized remote work tools and technology to collaborate with clients or teams.

2.2.6 Stay Proactive and Apply Strategically:

- **TAILOR YOUR APPLICATIONS:** Customize your application materials (cover letter, resume, or portfolio) for each remote job opportunity. Highlight relevant skills and experiences that align with the requirements of the specific remote position.

- **Follow up:** After submitting an application, follow up with the hiring manager or client to express your interest and inquire about the status of your application. This demonstrates your proactive approach and enthusiasm for the remote opportunity.

Conclusion:

LEVERAGING YOUR SKILLS to find remote work opportunities requires a proactive and strategic approach. Identify your marketable skills, research remote work industries and job boards, network effectively, polish your online presence, showcase your remote work competencies, and apply strategically to remote job opportunities. By leveraging your skills effectively, you can find remote work opportunities that align with your abilities and interests, enabling you to earn money online while enjoying the benefits of remote work.

2.3 Building a Freelance Portfolio and Personal Brand

BUILDING A FREELANCE portfolio and personal brand is essential for establishing credibility, attracting clients, and standing out in the competitive freelance market. In this section, we will explore strategies for creating a compelling freelance portfolio and developing a strong personal brand.

2.3.1 Define Your Focus and Target Audience:

- **IDENTIFY YOUR NICHE:** Determine the specific area or industry in which you excel and have a passion for. Focusing on a niche allows you to position yourself as an expert in that particular field.

- **Understand your target audience:** Research and understand the needs, preferences, and pain points of your target audience within your chosen niche. Tailor your portfolio and brand messaging to resonate with their specific requirements.

2.3.2 Showcase Your Best Work:

- **SELECT YOUR TOP PROJECTS:** Choose a selection of your best and most relevant work to showcase in your portfolio. Include a diverse range of projects that highlight your skills and demonstrate your ability to meet client objectives.

- **Create case studies:** Provide detailed case studies that explain the project scope, your approach, challenges faced, and the outcomes achieved. Include metrics, client testimonials, and any notable results to add credibility to your work.

2.3.3 Create an Engaging Portfolio Website:

- **DESIGN AND LAYOUT:** Develop a visually appealing and user-friendly portfolio website that aligns with your personal brand. Ensure it is easy to navigate, showcases your work prominently, and provides relevant information about your services.

- **About Me section:** Craft a compelling "About Me" page that introduces yourself, your background, and your expertise. Use this section to connect with potential clients on a personal level and convey your unique value proposition.

- **Contact information:** Make it easy for potential clients to get in touch with you by prominently displaying your contact information on your website. Include a contact form, email address, and links to your professional social media profiles.

2.3.4 Leverage Testimonials and Social Proof:

- **REQUEST CLIENT TESTIMONIALS:** Reach out to past clients and ask for testimonials that highlight their satisfaction with your work. Display these testimonials prominently on your portfolio website to build trust and credibility.

- **Showcase social proof:** If your work has been featured in reputable publications or you have received recognition or awards, include these achievements on your portfolio website. Social proof adds credibility and enhances your personal brand.

2.3.5 Develop a Consistent Personal Brand:

- **DEFINE YOUR BRAND identity:** Determine the key attributes, values, and qualities that define your personal brand. Develop a unique selling proposition (USP) that sets you apart from other freelancers in your niche.

- **Consistent visual branding:** Maintain a consistent visual identity across your portfolio website, social media profiles, and other online platforms. Use consistent colours, fonts, and visual elements that reflect your personal brand.

- **Authenticity and voice:** Infuse your personal brand with your authentic voice. Craft compelling and clear messaging that resonates with your target audience. Communicate your expertise, values, and the benefits clients can expect when working with you.

2.3.6 Network and Collaborate:

- **ENGAGE WITH YOUR INDUSTRY community:** Participate in industry-related forums, online groups, and social media communities. Share insights, offer help, and collaborate with other professionals in your niche. Networking can lead to valuable connections and potential client referrals.

- **Guest blogging and thought leadership:** Contribute guest blog posts or articles to reputable publications within your niche. This positions you as an expert and helps increase your visibility and reach within your target audience.

Conclusion:

BUILDING A FREELANCE portfolio and personal brand is essential for success in the freelance world. Define your focus, showcase your best work, and create a visually appealing portfolio website. Leverage testimonials, social proof, and consistent branding to build credibility and trust. Develop a unique personal brand that resonates with your target audience and allows you to stand out in the competitive freelance market. By investing time and effort in building a strong freelance portfolio and personal brand, you can attract clients and position yourself as a reputable and sought-after freelancer.

2.4 Negotiating Rates, Contracts, and Ensuring Timely Payments

NEGOTIATING RATES, establishing clear contracts, and ensuring timely payments are crucial aspects of freelance work. In this section, we will explore strategies for effectively negotiating rates, creating solid contracts, and managing payments to maintain a professional and profitable freelance business.

2.4.1 Determining Your Worth and Setting Rates:

- **RESEARCH INDUSTRY standards:** Conduct market research to understand the typical rates for freelance work in your industry and niche. This will provide a benchmark for setting your rates.

- **Consider your experience and expertise:** Take into account your level of experience, specialized skills, and the value you bring to clients when determining your rates. Clients are often willing to pay a premium for high-quality work from experienced freelancers.

- **Calculate your costs:** Consider your overhead expenses, taxes, and the time required to complete a project when setting your rates. Ensure that your rates allow you to cover your expenses and earn a fair income.

2.4.2 Effective Rate Negotiation:

- **FOCUS ON VALUE:** Emphasize the value you bring to the client's project. Highlight how your skills and expertise will help achieve their objectives, save them time, or improve their business.

- **Justify your rates:** Explain the reasons behind your rates, such as your experience, specialized knowledge, or the quality of your work. Provide examples of successful projects or client testimonials that demonstrate your value.

- **Offer options:** Instead of rigidly sticking to a single rate, provide clients with different pricing options that align with their budget. This flexibility can help you negotiate effectively and reach a mutually beneficial agreement.

2.4.3 Creating Clear and Comprehensive Contracts:

- **OUTLINE PROJECT SCOPE and deliverables:** Clearly define the scope of work, including the specific tasks, deadlines, and deliverables. This ensures that both you and the client have a shared understanding of the project's requirements.

- **Include payment terms:** Specify the payment structure, including the total project cost, payment milestones, and due dates. Outline your preferred payment method and any late payment penalties or fees.

- **Establish ownership and usage rights:** Clearly state who will retain ownership of the work and how it can be used by the client. Include any limitations or restrictions on the use of your work.

- **Seek legal advice if needed:** If you are dealing with complex projects or large clients, it may be wise to consult with a lawyer to ensure your contract protects your rights and interests.

2.4. 4 Managing Payments:

- **ESTABLISH CLEAR INVOICING procedures:** Clearly communicate your invoicing process to clients, including the format, frequency, and preferred method of receiving invoices.

- **Set expectations for payment terms:** Clearly state your payment terms in your contracts and ensure that clients understand their obligations. Specify due dates and any late payment penalties or interest charges.

- **Follow up on overdue payments:** If a client fails to make a payment on time, follow up promptly and professionally. Send polite reminders and inquire about the payment status. Be assertive in ensuring that you receive timely payments for your work.

- **Consider payment protection options:** Depending on the platform or freelance marketplace you are using, they may offer payment protection services or escrow systems. Familiarize yourself with these options to ensure your payments are secure.

2.4. 5 Professional Communication and Relationships:

- **MAINTAIN CLEAR AND professional communication:** Regularly update clients on project progress, address any concerns promptly, and be responsive to their inquiries or feedback. Clear and effective communication helps build trust and fosters positive client relationships.

- **Build long-term relationships:** Focus on building long-term relationships with clients by delivering high-quality work, exceeding expectations, and providing excellent customer service. Satisfied clients are more likely to hire you for future projects and refer you to others.

Conclusion:

NEGOTIATING RATES, creating solid contracts, and ensuring timely payments are essential for a successful freelance business. Research industry rates, effectively negotiate based on the value you bring, and clearly outline project details in contracts. Establish clear invoicing procedures and follow up on overdue payments professionally. By maintaining professional communication and building strong client relationships, you can establish yourself as a reliable and respected freelancer. These practices contribute to a thriving freelance business and pave the way for continued success in the online earning landscape.

2.5 Tips for Managing Clients and Delivering High-Quality Work

EFFECTIVELY MANAGING clients and delivering high-quality work are essential for maintaining successful freelance relationships and building a strong reputation. In this section, we will explore valuable tips to help you manage clients effectively and consistently deliver exceptional work.

2.5.1 Establish Clear Expectations:

- **SCOPE OF WORK:** Clearly define the scope of the project, including specific deliverables, deadlines, and any limitations or exclusions. This ensures that both you and the client have a shared understanding of the project's requirements.

- **Communication channels:** Establish preferred communication channels with clients, such as email, project management tools, or video calls. Clarify response times and availability to manage client expectations.

- **Revisions and feedback:** Set expectations for the number of revisions or feedback rounds included in the project. Clearly communicate how additional revisions or major changes may impact the project timeline and cost.

2.5.2 Regular and Transparent Communication:

- **PROACTIVE UPDATES:** Keep clients informed about the progress of their project regularly. Share updates on milestones achieved, challenges faced, and upcoming deadlines. Proactive communication helps build trust and reduces uncertainty.

- **Timely response:** Respond to client inquiries, messages, and feedback in a timely manner. Prompt and clear communication demonstrates professionalism and commitment to delivering a high-quality experience.

- **Seek clarification:** If you have any doubts or need clarification on project requirements, don't hesitate to ask. It's better to address any uncertainties upfront to ensure you are on the same page with the client.

2.5.3 Manage Deadlines and Prioritize Time Management:

- **SET REALISTIC DEADLINES:** When agreeing on project timelines, consider the scope of work and your availability. It's better to provide a realistic timeline upfront rather than overcommitting and potentially compromising quality.

- **Break down tasks:** Divide larger projects into smaller, manageable tasks with their own deadlines. This helps you stay organized and ensures that you make steady progress toward project completion.

- **Prioritize tasks:** Focus on important tasks and deliverables that align with client expectations and project objectives. Prioritizing effectively helps you manage your workload and meet deadlines without sacrificing quality.

2.5.4 Attention to Detail and Quality Control:

- **PROOFREAD AND REVIEW:** Ensure that your work is free from grammatical errors, typos, or inconsistencies. Take the time to proofread and review your work before submitting it to the client.

- **Quality assurance:** Implement quality control measures to ensure that the final deliverables meet or exceed client expectations. Double-check that all project requirements have been met and that the work is of high quality.

- **Delivering value-added work:** Go the extra mile by providing value-added suggestions, improvements, or insights related to the project. This demonstrates your expertise and commitment to delivering exceptional results.

2.5.5 Handle Feedback Professionally:

- **WELCOME FEEDBACK:** Embrace client feedback as an opportunity for growth and improvement. Be open to constructive criticism and use it to enhance your work and client satisfaction.

- **Address concerns promptly:** If a client expresses dissatisfaction or raises concerns, address them promptly and professionally. Listen actively, understand their perspective, and work collaboratively to find solutions.

- **Learn from feedback:** Reflect on feedback received and use it to improve your skills, processes, and client management approach. Continuous improvement based on feedback helps you deliver better work in the future.

2.5.6 Maintain Professionalism and Respect:

- **RESPECT DEADLINES and agreements:** Honor the commitments and deadlines established in contracts or agreements. Meeting deadlines consistently demonstrates reliability and professionalism.

- **Professional conduct:** Interact with clients in a professional and courteous manner. Be respectful, maintain confidentiality, and adhere to professional standards of communication and behaviour.

- **Handle conflicts professionally:** In the event of disagreements or conflicts, approach them with professionalism and diplomacy. Seek amicable resolutions and maintain a positive relationship with the client whenever possible.

Conclusion:

MANAGING CLIENTS EFFECTIVELY and consistently delivering high-quality work are essential for freelance success. Establish clear expectations, maintain regular and transparent communication, manage deadlines, and prioritize time management, pay attention to detail, and handle feedback professionally. By focusing on client satisfaction and consistently delivering exceptional work, you can build strong client relationships, secure repeat business, and enhance your reputation as a reliable and skilled freelancer. These practices contribute to a thriving freelance business in the online earning landscape.

CHAPTER CONCLUSION

FREELANCING AND REMOTE work offer exciting opportunities to earn money online while leveraging your skills and expertise. By exploring freelance platforms, building a freelance portfolio and personal brand, and effectively managing clients, you can thrive in the freelance world. Learn to negotiate rates and contracts, ensure timely payments, and deliver high-quality work to build a solid reputation and establish long-term client relationships. In the next chapters, we will delve into other specific online earning strategies and opportunities that you can explore.

Chapter 3: Monetizing Your Expertise

In this chapter, we will explore various ways to monetize your expertise and knowledge online. Whether you're an expert in a specific field, possess unique skills, or have valuable insights to share, there are opportunities to turn your expertise into a source of income. We will delve into creating and selling online courses, building a personal brand through blogging and content creation, launching a YouTube channel, hosting webinars and virtual workshops, and writing and self-publishing eBooks.

3.1 Creating and Selling Online Courses

CREATING AND SELLING online courses is a popular and effective way to monetize your expertise and share your knowledge with a global audience. In this section, we will delve into the process of creating and selling online courses, from planning and development to marketing and monetization.

3.1.1 Identify Your Expertise and Target Audience:

- **DEFINE YOUR AREA OF expertise:** Determine the subject or topic in which you possess deep knowledge, skills, and expertise. It could be anything from business and marketing to art, photography, fitness, or personal development.

- **Identify your target audience:** Understand who would benefit from your course. Consider their demographics, interests, skill levels, and learning objectives. This will help you tailor your course content to meet their specific needs.

3.1.2 Plan Your Course Content:

- **DEFINE YOUR LEARNING outcomes:** Clearly articulate the specific knowledge or skills participants will gain upon completing your course. Identify the learning objectives and goals you want to achieve with your course.

- **Structure your course:** Divide your course into logical modules or sections. Outline the topics you will cover in each module and determine the sequence that ensures a smooth learning progression.

- **Create engaging content:** Decide on the most suitable content formats for your course, such as video lessons, written materials, quizzes, assignments, downloadable resources, or interactive elements. Use a mix of formats to keep learners engaged and enhance their learning experience.

3.1.3 Choose an Online Course Platform:

- **RESEARCH ONLINE COURSE platforms:** Explore different online course platforms such as Udemy, Teachable, Thinkific, or Coursera. Evaluate their features, pricing, ease of use, marketing capabilities, and support options.

- **Select the right platform for your needs:** Consider factors like platform flexibility, customization options, payment processing, student engagement features, and marketing support. Choose a platform that aligns with your course goals and budget.

3.1.4 Develop High-Quality Course Content:

- **PREPARE COURSE MATERIALS:** Create well-structured course content that delivers on the learning outcomes you defined. Use clear and concise language, visual aids, and real-life examples to make your content engaging and relatable.

- **Record video lessons:** If you choose to include video lessons, invest in a good quality microphone, camera, and video editing software. Prepare scripts or outlines to ensure your video content is clear, organized, and professional.

- **Provide supplemental resources:** Enhance the learning experience by offering additional resources like PDF guides, checklists, templates, or recommended readings. These resources provide value and support learners in applying the concepts they learn.

3.1.5 Implement Assessments and Feedback:

- **DESIGN ASSESSMENTS:** Include quizzes, assignments, or practical exercises to assess learners' understanding and application of the course material. Design assessments that align with the learning outcomes and provide valuable feedback to learners.

- **Offer feedback and support:** Engage with your learners by providing feedback on their assignments or responding to their questions and comments promptly. This helps create a sense of community and encourages active participation.

3.1.6 Market and Promote Your Course:

- **CRAFT A COMPELLING course description:** Write a clear and compelling course description that highlights the benefits, learning outcomes, and value participants will gain from taking your course. Use persuasive language to grab the attention of potential learners.

- **Leverage your network:** Tap into your existing network, such as social media connections, email contacts, or professional communities, to promote your course. Ask for testimonials or endorsements from satisfied learners to build credibility.

- **Utilize digital marketing strategies:** Utilize digital marketing techniques like content marketing, social media promotion, email marketing, and paid advertising to reach a wider audience. Create engaging content related to your course topic and share it across various platforms to attract potential learners.

- **Offer limited-time promotions or discounts:** Create a sense of urgency and incentivize enrolment by offering limited-time promotions or early-bird discounts. This can help generate initial interest and encourage learners to take action.

3.1.7 Monetize Your Course:

- **SET A COMPETITIVE price:** Research similar courses in your niche to determine a fair and competitive price for your course. Consider factors like the value provided, course length, the depth of content, and your level of expertise.

- **Consider different pricing models:** Explore various pricing models such as one-time payments, monthly subscriptions, or tiered pricing options based on the level of access or additional resources provided.

- **Offer bundled packages:** Increase the perceived value of your course by bundling it with additional resources, coaching sessions, or exclusive bonuses. This can entice learners to choose your course over alternatives.

- **Continuously improve and update:** Gather feedback from your learners and use it to improve your course. Regularly update your course content to ensure it stays relevant and up to date in a fast-changing world.

Conclusion:

CREATING AND SELLING online courses allows you to monetize your expertise, reach a global audience, and make a meaningful impact through education. By identifying your expertise, planning your course content, selecting the right platform, developing high-quality content, implementing assessments, marketing your course effectively, and monetizing it appropriately, you can build a successful online course business. Remember to continuously engage with learners, gather feedback, and refine your course to ensure a positive learning experience.

3.2 Building a Personal Brand through Blogging and Content Creation

BUILDING A PERSONAL brand through blogging and content creation is an effective way to establish yourself as an expert in your field, share valuable insights, and attract a dedicated audience. In this section, we will explore the steps involved in building a personal brand through blogging and content creation.

3.2.1 Define Your Niche and Target Audience:

- **IDENTIFY YOUR EXPERTISE and passions:** Determine the specific area or topic in which you excel and have a genuine interest. Choose a niche that allows you to showcase your expertise and aligns with your target audience's needs.

- **Define your target audience:** Understand the demographics, interests, and pain points of your target audience. This will help you tailor your content to resonate with them and provide solutions to their problems.

3.2.2 Create a Compelling Blog:

- **CHOOSE A BLOGGING platform:** Select a reliable and user-friendly blogging platform such as WordPress, Blogger, or Medium. Consider your specific needs, technical skills, and customization options when making your choice.

- **Define your brand identity:** Establish a clear and consistent brand identity for your blog. Determine your unique selling proposition (USP), visual style, voice, and tone. Ensure that your brand aligns with your expertise and appeals to your target audience.

- **Develop high-quality content:** Create valuable, well-researched, and engaging content that addresses your audience's pain points, provides solutions, and offers insights. Utilize various content formats, such as articles, guides, tutorials, infographics, or videos, to cater to different learning preferences.

3.2.3 Optimize for Search Engines:

- **PERFORM KEYWORD RESEARCH:** Identify relevant keywords and phrases that are commonly searched by your target audience. Use keyword research tools like Google Keyword Planner or SEMrush to find popular and relevant keywords.

- **Optimize your content:** Incorporate your target keywords naturally into your blog posts, titles, headings, and meta descriptions. Write compelling and descriptive meta titles and descriptions to attract search engine users to click on your content.

- **Focus on quality and relevance:** Ensure that your content is well-written, informative, and valuable to your audience. High-quality content that satisfies user intent and provides a great user experience tends to rank higher in search engine results.

3.2.4 Promote Your Blog:

- **UTILIZE SOCIAL MEDIA platforms:** Leverage social media channels that align with your target audience to promote your blog and build a community. Share your blog posts, engage with your followers, and participate in relevant discussions.

- **Guest blogging:** Contribute guest posts to reputable websites, blogs, or publications within your niche. This allows you to tap into existing audiences and establish your credibility as an expert in your field.

- **Collaborate with influencers:** Partner with influencers or experts in your industry for collaborations, interviews, or joint content creation. This can help you reach a wider audience and gain exposure within your target market.

- **Engage with your audience:** Respond to comments, messages, and feedback from your readers. Engage in meaningful conversations, address their questions, and show appreciation for their support. Building relationships with your audience fosters loyalty and encourages them to share your content.

3.2.5 Monetize Your Blog:

- **DISPLAY ADVERTISEMENTS:** Join ad networks like Google AdSense or Mediavine to display relevant ads on your blog. Earn revenue based on ad impressions or clicks. However, be mindful of maintaining a balance between ads and user experience.

- **Affiliate marketing:** Partner with relevant companies and promote their products or services through affiliate links. Earn a commission for each referral or sale generated through your affiliate links.

- **Sponsored content:** Collaborate with brands and create sponsored content that aligns with your blog and resonates with your audience. Be transparent with your readers about sponsored content and maintain authenticity.

- **Create and sell digital products:** Develop and sell digital products like e-books, online courses, templates, or digital downloads that offer additional value to your audience. Leverage your expertise to provide solutions to their needs.

3.2.6 Continuously Engage and Evolve:

- **CONSISTENCY AND REGULARITY:** Publish content consistently to maintain engagement with your audience. Develop an editorial calendar and stick to a regular posting schedule.

- **Listen to your audience:** Pay attention to the feedback and preferences of your readers. Analyse metrics, such as website analytics and social media insights, to gain insights into their preferences and adjust your content strategy accordingly.

- **Evolve and adapt:** Stay updated with industry trends, emerging topics, and changes in your niche. Continuously expand your knowledge, explore new content formats, and adapt your strategy to meet the evolving needs of your audience.

Conclusion:

BUILDING A PERSONAL brand through blogging and content creation allows you to showcase your expertise, connect with your target audience, and monetize your knowledge. Define your niche, create compelling content, optimize for search engines, promote your blog through various channels, and monetize your efforts through advertisements, affiliate marketing, sponsored content, or digital products. Remember to engage with your audience, listen to their feedback, and adapt your strategy as needed. By consistently delivering valuable content and building a loyal following, you can establish a strong personal brand and generate income from your blog.

3.3 Launching a YouTube Channel and Leveraging Video Content

LAUNCHING A YOUTUBE channel and leveraging video content is an effective way to build a personal brand, reach a global audience, and monetize your expertise. In this section, we will explore the steps involved in launching a successful YouTube channel and maximizing the potential of video content.

3.3.1 Define Your Channel's Focus and Target Audience:

- **CHOOSE YOUR NICHE:** Determine the specific area or topic that your YouTube channel will focus on. Consider your expertise, interests, and the needs of your target audience.

- **Identify your target audience:** Understand the demographics, interests, and preferences of your target audience. Tailor your content to provide value and meet their specific needs.

3.3.2 Set Up Your YouTube Channel:

- **CREATE A YOUTUBE ACCOUNT:** Sign up for a YouTube account using your Google account. Customize your channel name, profile picture, and channel art to reflect your brand identity.

- **Develop a channel trailer:** Create a compelling channel trailer that introduces yourself, your content, and the value you provide to viewers. Use this opportunity to capture the attention of new visitors and encourage them to subscribe.

3.3.3 Plan and Produce Engaging Video Content:

- **DEFINE YOUR CONTENT strategy:** Determine the types of videos you will create, such as tutorials, educational content, vlogs, interviews, reviews, or entertainment. Develop a content calendar to ensure consistency and variety.

- **Create high-quality videos:** Invest in good quality audio and video equipment, such as a microphone and camera, to produce professional-looking videos. Pay attention to lighting, background, and overall production quality.

- **Script or outline your videos:** Plan the structure and key points of each video to ensure clarity and coherence. While some creators prefer scripting every word, others find outlining the main talking points to be more effective and natural.

3.3.4 Optimize Your Videos for Discovery:

- **CONDUCT KEYWORD RESEARCH:** Identify relevant keywords and phrases related to your content. Use tools like Google Keyword Planner, VidIQ, or TubeBuddy to find keywords with search volume and optimize your video titles, descriptions, and tags accordingly.

- **Eye-catching thumbnails:** Create visually appealing and attention-grabbing video thumbnails. Use clear and engaging visuals, text overlays, and branding elements to entice viewers to click on your videos.

- **Encourage engagement:** Prompt viewers to like, comment, and subscribe to your channel. Ask questions, encourage discussion, and respond to comments to foster engagement and build a loyal community.

3.3.5 Promote Your Channel and Collaborate with Others:

- **SHARE ON SOCIAL MEDIA:** Promote your YouTube channel and videos on your social media platforms to reach a wider audience. Share teasers, snippets, or behind-the-scenes content to create anticipation and encourage viewers to visit your channel.

- **Collaborate with other creators:** Collaborate with other YouTube creators within your niche to create joint videos, interviews, or collaborations. This cross-promotion can help you reach new audiences and gain exposure.

3.3.6 Monetize Your Channel:

- **APPLY FOR THE YOUTUBE Partner Program:** Once you meet the eligibility requirements, apply for the YouTube Partner Program to monetize your channel. This allows you to earn revenue through advertisements, channel memberships, Super Chat, and YouTube Premium revenue.

- **Brand partnerships and sponsored content:** Collaborate with brands and create sponsored content that aligns with your channel's niche and resonates with your audience. Be transparent about sponsored content and maintain authenticity.

- **Sell merchandise:** Utilize the YouTube Merch Shelf feature to sell branded merchandise directly from your channel. Create and promote merchandise that reflects your brand and appeals to your audience.

3.3.7 Engage with Your Audience and Analyze Performance:

- **RESPOND TO COMMENTS and interact with your audience:** Engage with your viewers by responding to comments, asking for feedback, and incorporating their suggestions into future videos. Building a strong relationship with your audience fosters loyalty and encourages them to become active participants.

- **Analyse video performance:** Utilize YouTube Analytics to understand your audience's preferences, video engagement, and audience retention. Analyse the metrics to identify trends, improve your content strategy, and create videos that resonate with your viewers.

Conclusion:

LAUNCHING A YOUTUBE channel and leveraging video content offers tremendous potential for building a personal brand and monetizing your expertise. Define your channel's focus, produce high-quality videos, optimize them for discovery, promote your channel through various channels, collaborate with others, and monetize your efforts through the YouTube Partner Program, brand partnerships, sponsored content, or merchandise sales. Engage with your audience, analyse video performance, and adapt your content strategy to meet the evolving needs and preferences of your viewers. By consistently delivering valuable video content and building a loyal subscriber base, you can establish a successful YouTube channel and leverage the power of video to monetize your expertise.

3.4 Hosting Webinars and Virtual Workshops

HOSTING WEBINARS AND virtual workshops is an effective way to share your expertise, engage with your audience in real-time, and monetize your knowledge. In this section, we will explore the steps involved in hosting successful webinars and virtual workshops.

3.4.1 Define Your Webinar or Workshop Topic

and Format:

- **CHOOSE A TOPIC:** Determine the subject or skill you want to teach through your webinar or virtual workshop. Select a topic that aligns with your expertise and addresses the needs and interests of your target audience.

- **Decide on the format:** Determine the format that best suits your topic and audience. Options include lecture-style presentations, interactive workshops, panel discussions, Q&A sessions, or a combination of formats.

3.4.2 Select a Webinar or Virtual Workshop Platform:

- **RESEARCH WEBINAR PLATFORMS:** Explore different webinar platforms such as Zoom, WebEx, GoToWebinar, or Livestorm. Consider features like participant limits, interactive tools, recording options, and integration capabilities.

- **Choose the right platform:** Select a platform that aligns with your technical requirements, budget, and audience size. Ensure that the platform provides a user-friendly experience for both hosts and participants.

3.4.3 Plan and Prepare Your Content:

- **OUTLINE YOUR PRESENTATION:** Structure your webinar or virtual workshop with a clear introduction, main content sections, and a conclusion. Create an engaging storyline that guides participants through the learning experience.

- **Develop visual aids:** Create visually appealing slides, graphics, or multimedia elements to support your presentation. Use visuals to enhance understanding, reinforce key points, and maintain participant engagement.

- **Prepare resources and handouts:** Gather relevant resources, worksheets, checklists, or handouts that participants can download or access during the webinar or workshop. These materials provide additional value and help participants apply what they learn.

3.4.4 Promote Your Webinar or Workshop:

- **DEVELOP A MARKETING plan:** Identify your target audience and create a promotional strategy to reach them. Utilize email marketing, social media platforms, your website or blog, industry networks, and collaborations with influencers to generate interest and registrations.

- **Create compelling promotional materials:** Design visually appealing graphics, write persuasive copy, and communicate the benefits and value participants will gain from attending your webinar or virtual workshop.

- **Use landing pages or registration forms:** Create a dedicated landing page or registration form that captures participant information and allows them to sign up for the event. Collect relevant details like name, email address, and any pre-webinar survey questions.

3.4.5 Conducting the Webinar or Workshop:

- **PREPARE THE TECHNOLOGY and setup:** Ensure that you have a stable internet connection, a quality microphone, and webcam for clear communication. Test your equipment, platform settings, and any screen sharing or interactive tools before the event.

- **Engage participants:** Begin with a warm welcome, introduce yourself, and set expectations for the session. Encourage active participation through polls, chat functions, or Q&A sessions. Maintain a conversational tone and address participant questions or comments throughout the session.

- **Deliver valuable content:** Share your expertise, insights, and practical tips during the webinar or virtual workshop. Present information in a clear and organized manner, focusing on delivering value to the participants.

- **Incorporate interactive elements:** Include interactive activities, group discussions, or breakout rooms to encourage participant engagement and peer-to-peer learning. These activities help participants apply what they learn and enhance the overall experience.

- **Allow time for questions:** Allocate time for participants to ask questions and provide clarifications. Address their inquiries, offer insights, and encourage discussion to foster an interactive learning environment.

3.4.6 Follow-Up and Engagement:

- **SEND POST-EVENT FOLLOW-up emails:** Send a thank-you email to all participants, including any promised resources, links to recordings, or additional materials. Seek feedback through surveys to gather insights for improving future webinars or workshops.

- **Engage with attendees after the event:** Continue the conversation by encouraging participants to connect with you on social media or join your email list. Share related content, follow up with additional resources, or offer special promotions to maintain engagement.

3.4.7 Monetization and Future Opportunities:

- **CHARGE FOR PARTICIPATION:** Consider charging a fee for attending your webinars or virtual workshops, especially if they offer substantial value or exclusive content. Determine a fair price based on the value you provide and the market demand.

- **Upsell additional products or services:** Utilize webinars or workshops as an opportunity to promote and sell your other products, services, or courses. Offer special discounts or exclusive offers to participants, encouraging them to take the next step.

- **Repurpose content:** Record your webinars or workshops and repurpose them into on-demand content or future courses. This allows you to extend the lifespan of your content and reach a wider audience.

Conclusion:

HOSTING WEBINARS AND virtual workshops is an effective way to share your expertise, engage with your audience, and monetize your knowledge. Define your topic, select a suitable platform, plan, and prepare your content, promote your event, deliver valuable content, engage participants, and follow up after the event. By hosting successful webinars and virtual workshops, you can establish yourself as an authority in your field, generate income, and open opportunities for future collaboration and growth.

3.5 Writing and Self-Publishing eBooks

WRITING AND SELF-PUBLISHING eBooks is a popular method to monetize your expertise, reach a wide audience, and establish yourself as an authority in your field. In this section, we will explore the steps involved in writing and self-publishing eBooks.

3.5.1 Choose Your eBook Topic:

- **IDENTIFY YOUR EXPERTISE:** Determine the subject or niche in which you possess deep knowledge and expertise. Consider your passions, professional experience, or specialized skills when selecting your eBook topic.

- **Research market demand:** Conduct market research to validate the demand for your chosen topic. Look for existing eBooks or publications in your niche to assess competition and identify opportunities to offer unique value.

3.5.2 Plan and Outline Your eBook:

- **DEFINE YOUR EBOOK'S purpose:** Determine the primary objective of your eBook. Will it be informative, instructional, inspirational, or a combination? Clarify the key message or problem you intend to address for your readers.

- **Outline your eBook:** Create a clear and organized structure for your eBook by outlining chapters, sections, or key concepts. This provides a roadmap for your writing process and ensures a logical flow of information.

3.5.3 Write and Edit Your eBook:

- **START WRITING:** Begin writing your eBook based on your outlined structure. Focus on creating valuable and engaging content that resonates with your target audience. Write in a conversational tone to establish a connection with your readers.

- **Edit and proofread:** Review and revise your content for clarity, coherence, grammar, and spelling errors. Consider seeking assistance from professional editors or beta readers to ensure a polished final product.

3.5.4 Design and Format Your eBook:

- **CREATE A PROFESSIONAL cover design:** Design an eye-catching and visually appealing eBook cover that reflects the topic, tone, and branding of your eBook. Utilize design software or hire a professional designer to create a high-quality cover.

- **Format your eBook:** Ensure your eBook is properly formatted for various reading devices, such as Kindle, Nook, or PDF. Pay attention to font styles, spacing, headings, and any images or graphics. You can use eBook formatting software like Calibre or hire a professional formatter for this task.

3.5.5 Self-Publish Your eBook:

- **CHOOSE A SELF-PUBLISHING platform:** Select a self-publishing platform that suits your needs, such as Amazon Kindle Direct Publishing (KDP), Smashwords, or Apple Books. Each platform has its own requirements and distribution options.

- **Prepare your eBook for publishing:** Follow the guidelines provided by the self-publishing platform to upload your eBook file, cover image, book description, and other necessary information. Provide accurate metadata and select appropriate categories and keywords for discoverability.

- **Set the price:** Determine the pricing strategy for your eBook. Consider factors like the length, value, competition, and target market. Experiment with different price points or promotional discounts to attract readers.

3.5.6 Market and Promote Your eBook:

- **DEVELOP A MARKETING plan:** Outline a marketing strategy to create awareness and generate interest in your eBook. Consider utilizing social media, your website or blog, email marketing, guest blogging, or collaborations with influencers to reach your target audience.

- **Leverage your network:** Utilize your personal and professional networks to promote your eBook. Encourage friends, colleagues, and readers to spread the word and leave reviews on platforms like Amazon to boost credibility.

- **Offer limited-time promotions:** Generate excitement and urgency by offering limited-time promotions or discounts for your eBook. Leverage these promotions to attract new readers and encourage them to take action.

3.5.7 Engage with Readers and Gather Feedback:

- **ENCOURAGE READER REVIEWS:** Request honest reviews from readers who have purchased and read your eBook. Positive reviews can increase visibility and credibility, while constructive feedback helps you improve future editions or publications.

- **Engage with readers:** Interact with your readers through comments, emails, or social media channels. Respond to their questions, provide additional resources, and build a community around your eBook.

3.5.8 Explore Additional Opportunities:

- **CREATE RELATED CONTENT:** Leverage your eBook's content to create additional related content, such as blog posts, videos, or online courses. This allows you to repurpose your knowledge and reach a wider audience.

- **Consider translations or audio versions:** Explore the possibility of translating your eBook into different languages or creating an audiobook version. These formats can expand your reach and attract new readers.

Conclusion:

WRITING AND SELF-PUBLISHING eBooks provide an opportunity to share your expertise, monetize your knowledge, and establish yourself as an authority in your field. Choose a compelling topic, plan, and outline your eBook, write and edit your content, design and format your eBook professionally, self-publish on suitable platforms, and market your eBook effectively. Engage with your readers, gather feedback, and explore additional opportunities to leverage your eBook's content. By following these steps and continuously improving your craft, you can successfully write and self-publish eBooks that resonate with your audience and contribute to your online earning journey.

CHAPTER CONCLUSION

MONETIZING YOUR EXPERTISE offers a rewarding way to earn income online while sharing your knowledge with others. Consider creating and selling online courses, building a personal brand through blogging and content creation, launching a YouTube channel, hosting webinars and virtual workshops, and writing and self-publishing eBooks. Each method has its unique advantages and requires consistent effort, quality content, and effective marketing to succeed. Choose the strategies that align with your strengths and interests, and adapt them to your target audience. By monetizing your expertise, you can establish yourself as a thought leader, grow your online presence, and generate income from sharing your valuable knowledge.

Chapter 4: Affiliate Marketing and Influencer Strategies

In this chapter, we will explore the world of affiliate marketing and influencer strategies. Affiliate marketing allows you to earn a commission by promoting products or services of other companies, while influencer strategies leverage your online presence and audience to collaborate with brands. We will dive into the basics of affiliate marketing, choosing profitable affiliate programs, building an engaged audience, promoting affiliate products on social media, and developing partnerships with brands as an influencer.

4.1 Understanding the Basics of Affiliate Marketing

AFFILIATE MARKETING is a performance-based marketing strategy where you earn a commission for promoting and generating sales or actions for a company's products or services. It allows you to monetize your online presence and leverage your influence to drive traffic and conversions for brands. Here are the key components and concepts to understand:

4.1.1 Roles in Affiliate Marketing:

- **MERCHANT OR ADVERTISER:** The company or business that offers products or services and establishes an affiliate program to promote them.

- **Affiliate or publisher:** The individual or entity that promotes the merchant's products or services through various marketing channels.

4.1.2 Affiliate Networks and Programs:

- **AFFILIATE NETWORKS:** These platforms act as intermediaries between merchants and affiliates. They provide a centralized marketplace where affiliates can find and join multiple affiliate programs from different merchants.

- **Affiliate programs:** These are specific programs created by individual merchants to manage their affiliate partnerships. They offer unique tracking links or codes that affiliates use to promote their products or services.

4.1.3 Affiliate Links and Tracking:

- **AFFILIATE LINKS:** These are unique URLs assigned to each affiliate to track the traffic and sales they generate. When a user clicks on an affiliate link and makes a purchase or completes a desired action, the affiliate is credited with a commission.

- **Tracking cookies:** Affiliate links often contain tracking cookies that are stored on the user's browser. These cookies help track the user's activity and attribute any subsequent purchases to the affiliate, even if the user doesn't make an immediate purchase.

4.1.4 Commission Structures:

- **PERCENTAGE-BASED COMMISSION:** Affiliates earn a percentage of the total sale amount. For example, if the commission rate is 10% and the sale is $100, the affiliate earns $10.

- **Flat-rate commission:** Affiliates earn a fixed amount for each referred sale or action. For instance, if the commission is $20 per sale, the affiliate earns $20 regardless of the sale amount.

- **Performance-based commission:** Some affiliate programs offer tiered commission structures, where affiliates earn higher rates based on the number of sales or actions they generate.

4.1.5 Affiliate Marketing Strategies:

- **CONTENT MARKETING:** Creating high-quality content such as blog posts, articles, or videos that provide value to your audience and incorporate affiliate links within the content.

- **Social media marketing:** Promoting affiliate products through your social media channels, sharing personal recommendations, and engaging with your followers.

- **Email marketing:** Utilizing your email list to share product recommendations, exclusive offers, or promotions with your subscribers.

- **Review and comparison websites:** Creating websites that review or compare products and include affiliate links to drive traffic and conversions.

- **Influencer marketing:** Collaborating with brands as an influencer to promote their products or services to your audience.

4.1.6 Compliance and Disclosure:

- **FTC GUIDELINES:** In many countries, including the United States, the Federal Trade Commission (FTC) has guidelines that require affiliates to disclose their relationship with the promoted products or services. This disclosure ensures transparency and helps maintain trust with your audience.

- **Disclosure methods:** Disclosures can be made through statements like "This post contains affiliate links" or using specific disclosure labels or hashtags, such as #ad or #sponsored.

Conclusion:

UNDERSTANDING THE BASICS of affiliate marketing is crucial for successfully monetizing your online presence. By joining affiliate networks or programs, using unique affiliate links, tracking cookies, and implementing various marketing strategies, you can earn commissions for driving sales and actions for brands. Remember to comply with FTC guidelines and disclose your affiliate relationships to maintain transparency with your audience. With consistent effort, strategic promotions, and valuable content, you can thrive in the world of affiliate marketing.

4.2 Choosing Profitable Affiliate Programs and Products

CHOOSING PROFITABLE affiliate programs and products is essential to maximize your earnings and ensure a successful affiliate marketing venture. Here are some steps to help you select the right affiliate programs and products:

4.2.1 Identify Your Niche and Target Audience:

- **DETERMINE YOUR NICHE:** Define the specific area or topic in which you have expertise and are passionate about. Focusing on a niche allows you to target a specific audience and build credibility in that area.

- **Understand your target audience:** Conduct market research to identify the demographics, interests, and needs of your target audience.

This understanding will help you choose affiliate programs and products that align with their preferences.

4.2.2 Research Affiliate Programs:

- **EXPLORE REPUTABLE** affiliate networks: Join established affiliate networks such as Amazon Associates, ClickBank, ShareASale, or CJ Affiliate. These networks offer a wide range of affiliate programs across various industries.

- **Consider the commission structure:** Look for programs that offer competitive commission rates. Compare the commission percentages or flat-rate commissions offered by different programs to determine their earning potential.

- **Evaluate program credibility and track record:** Research the reputation of the affiliate programs you are considering. Read reviews, check for payment reliability, and ensure they have a solid track record of affiliate support and timely payouts.

- **Review program terms and conditions:** Carefully read the program's terms and conditions to understand any restrictions or limitations. Pay attention to cookie duration (the length of time affiliate referrals is tracked) and any exclusive promotional requirements.

4.2.3 Assess Product Quality and Demand:

- **CHOOSE HIGH-QUALITY** products or services: Select affiliate products that are reputable, reliable, and provide value to customers. Research customer reviews, ratings, and feedback to ensure product quality.

- **Assess market demand:** Analyse the market demand for the products you are considering. Look for products with a sizable target audience, high search volume, and a demonstrated need. This ensures that there is sufficient demand and potential for conversions.

- **Consider product relevance to your audience:** Ensure that the affiliate products or services you promote align with the interests, needs, and preferences of your target audience. Promoting relevant products enhances trust and increases the likelihood of conversions.

4.2.4 Check Affiliate Support and Resources:

- **EVALUATE AFFILIATE support:** Assess the level of support provided by the affiliate program. Look for resources such as marketing materials, promotional tools, tracking dashboards, and dedicated affiliate managers who can assist you.

- **Access marketing materials:** Determine if the program provides banners, product images, text links, or other marketing assets that you can utilize in your promotions. These materials can save time and enhance the visual appeal of your affiliate content.

4.2.5 Analyse Earnings Potential:

- **ESTIMATE POTENTIAL earnings:** Consider the average sale amount, commission rate, and conversion rates for the affiliate products. Estimate potential earnings based on your audience size, reach, and promotional efforts.

- **Look for upsell or recurring commission opportunities:** Some affiliate programs offer upsell or recurring commission structures. These can lead to higher earnings as customers make additional purchases or subscribe to ongoing services.

4.2.6 Consider Long-Term Partnerships:

- **FOCUS ON SUSTAINABLE affiliate partnerships:** Look for programs and products that have a long-term potential for consistent earnings. Building strong relationships with reliable merchants can lead to future collaboration opportunities and higher commission rates.

- **Monitor program performance:** Regularly assess the performance of your chosen affiliate programs and products. Track conversion rates, earnings, and customer feedback to ensure they align with your expectations.

Conclusion:

CHOOSING PROFITABLE affiliate programs and products requires careful consideration of your niche, target audience, program credibility, product quality, demand, support, and potential earnings. By conducting thorough research, analysing market trends, and aligning your promotions with the needs of your audience, you can select affiliate programs and products that maximize your earnings potential and contribute to a successful affiliate marketing journey.

4.3 Building an Engaged Audience and Growing Your Online Presence

BUILDING AN ENGAGED audience and growing your online presence is crucial for a successful affiliate marketing venture. Here are some strategies to help you build a loyal following and expand your online reach:

4.3.1 Define Your Target Audience:

- **IDENTIFY YOUR NICHE:** Determine the specific area or topic in which you have expertise and want to focus on. This helps you tailor your content and promotions to a specific audience.

- **Understand your audience:** Conduct market research to understand the demographics, interests, preferences, and pain points of your target audience. This knowledge will guide your content creation and promotional strategies.

4.3.2 Create High-Quality and Valuable Content:

- **PROVIDE VALUABLE INFORMATION:** Create content that educates, informs, entertains, or solves a problem for your audience. Offer unique insights, tips, tutorials, or industry updates that showcase your expertise and provide value.

- **Consistency is key:** Regularly publish high-quality content to keep your audience engaged. Set a content schedule and stick to it. This could be blog posts, videos, podcasts, social media updates, or a combination, depending on your platform.

- **Optimize for SEO:** Research relevant keywords and incorporate them strategically into your content to improve its search engine visibility. This helps attract organic traffic and expands your reach.

4.3.3 Engage with Your Audience:

- **RESPOND TO COMMENTS and messages:** Actively engage with your audience by responding to comments, messages, and inquiries. Encourage conversation, answer questions, and show appreciation for their feedback.

- **Foster a sense of community:** Create a welcoming and inclusive environment where your audience feels comfortable engaging with you and each other. Encourage discussions, ask for opinions, and facilitate interactions among your followers.

- **Utilize social media platforms:** Leverage social media platforms such as Instagram, Facebook, Twitter, or LinkedIn to interact with your audience. Post engaging content, respond to comments, and participate in relevant communities and discussions.

4.3.4 Build an Email List:

- **OFFER VALUABLE INCENTIVES:** Provide a compelling reason for your audience to join your email list, such as exclusive content, discounts, or freebies related to your niche. This helps capture their email addresses and builds a direct line of communication.

- **Send regular newsletters:** Send informative and engaging newsletters to your email list. Share updates, new content, promotions, and affiliate product recommendations to nurture the relationship with your subscribers.

4.3.5 Collaborate with Other Influencers and Brands:

- **CROSS-PROMOTION:** Collaborate with other influencers or content creators in your niche to cross-promote each other's content. This exposes your brand to new audiences and helps you reach a wider network.

- **Guest posting:** Write guest posts for popular blogs or platforms in your niche. This allows you to tap into their existing audience and establish yourself as an authority in the field.

- **Brand partnerships:** Develop partnerships with relevant brands in your niche. Collaborate on sponsored content or affiliate promotions that align with your audience's interests. These partnerships can expand your reach and provide additional monetization opportunities.

4.3.6 Leverage Analytics and Insights:

- **MONITOR AND ANALYSE data:** Utilize analytics tools to track the performance of your content, website, or social media channels. Pay attention to metrics such as engagement rates, website traffic, conversion rates, and audience demographics. Use these insights to refine your strategies and optimize your content.

Conclusion:

BUILDING AN ENGAGED audience and growing your online presence are essential for a successful affiliate marketing journey. By defining your target audience, creating valuable content, engaging with your audience, building an email list, collaborating with influencers and brands, and leveraging analytics, you can foster a loyal following and expand your reach. Remember to stay consistent, provide value, and adapt your strategies based on audience feedback and market trends. With dedication and strategic efforts, you can build a strong online presence that supports your affiliate marketing goals.

4.4 Leveraging Social Media Platforms to Promote Affiliate Products

SOCIAL MEDIA PLATFORMS provide a powerful avenue to promote affiliate products, reach a wider audience, and drive conversions. Here are some strategies to effectively leverage social media for affiliate marketing:

4.4.1 Choose the Right Social Media Platforms:

- **IDENTIFY YOUR TARGET audience:** Determine the social media platforms where your target audience is most active. Focus your efforts on platforms where you can effectively engage with and reach your desired audience.

- **Research platform features:** Understand the features and capabilities of each social media platform. For example, Instagram is highly visual, YouTube allows for longer video content, and Twitter is known for real-time updates and conversations. Choose platforms that align with your content format and audience preferences.

4.4.2 Create Compelling Content:

- **SHOWCASE PRODUCT BENEFITS:** Highlight the key benefits, features, or unique selling points of the affiliate products in your content. Demonstrate how the products solve a problem or improve the lives of your audience.

- **Utilize high-quality visuals:** Incorporate visually appealing images, graphics, or videos to capture attention and enhance the appeal of your content. Use professional-looking visuals that align with your brand and the products you promote.

- **Incorporate storytelling:** Craft compelling stories around the affiliate products to engage your audience emotionally. Share personal experiences, case studies, or testimonials to add authenticity and build trust.

4.4.3 Share Genuine Recommendations:

- **USE PERSONAL EXPERIENCES:** Provide honest and genuine recommendations based on your personal experiences with the affiliate products. Your audience will appreciate authentic endorsements and trust your recommendations.

- **Transparently disclose affiliate partnerships:** Clearly disclose your affiliate relationships in your social media posts. Use labels such as "#ad," "#sponsored," or "affiliate link" to maintain transparency and comply with regulatory guidelines.

4.4.4 Engage and Interact with Your Audience:

- **RESPOND TO COMMENTS and messages:** Actively engage with your audience by responding to comments, answering questions, and acknowledging their feedback. Show genuine interest in their opinions and foster two-way communication.

- **Encourage user-generated content:** Encourage your followers to share their experiences with the affiliate products. This can be through reviews, testimonials, or using specific hashtags related to the products. Repost or feature user-generated content to showcase social proof and encourage engagement.

4.4.5 Strategic Call-to-Actions:

- **USE CLEAR AND PERSUASIVE call-to-actions (CTAs):** Encourage your audience to take action by incorporating clear CTAs in your social media posts. Direct them to click on a link, make a purchase, or sign up for a service using your affiliate link.

- **Offer exclusive promotions or discounts:** Create a sense of urgency and incentive by offering exclusive promotions or discounts to your audience. Communicate the limited-time nature of the offer to encourage immediate action.

4.4.6 Track and Optimize Performance:

- **MONITOR ANALYTICS and metrics:** Utilize social media analytics tools to track the performance of your affiliate marketing efforts. Analyse engagement rates, click-through rates, conversions, and audience demographics to identify trends and optimize your strategies.

- **A/B testing:** Experiment with different content formats, visuals, CTAs, and posting times to identify what resonates best with your audience. Test and refine your approach based on the insights you gather.

4.4.7 Compliance and Disclosure:

- **FOLLOW DISCLOSURE guidelines:** Comply with regulations and platform policies by clearly disclosing your affiliate relationships in accordance with FTC guidelines or the respective platform's requirements. Use appropriate labels or hashtags to disclose sponsored or affiliate content.

Conclusion:

LEVERAGING SOCIAL MEDIA platforms effectively can significantly boost your affiliate marketing efforts. Choose the right platforms for your target audience, create compelling content, provide genuine recommendations, engage with your audience, use persuasive CTAs, track performance, and comply with disclosure guidelines. By strategically leveraging social media, you can reach a wider audience, build trust, and drive conversions for the affiliate products you promote.

4.5 Developing Partnerships with Brands as an Influencer

DEVELOPING PARTNERSHIPS with brands as an influencer can provide exciting opportunities for collaboration, increased visibility, and monetization. Here are some steps to help you establish successful brand partnerships:

4.5.1 Define Your Niche and Brand Identity:

- **IDENTIFY YOUR NICHE:** Determine the specific area or topic in which you have expertise and a dedicated audience. Focusing on a niche allows you to position yourself as an authority and attract brands that align with your content.

- **Define your brand identity:** Establish a clear and consistent brand identity that reflects your values, personality, and unique selling proposition. This helps brands understand your audience and whether you are a good fit for their products or services.

4.5.2 Create Compelling Content:

- **SHOWCASE YOUR EXPERTISE:** Create high-quality and engaging content that demonstrates your knowledge, skills, and unique perspective. This content should resonate with your audience and align with the brand's values.

- **Highlight your audience engagement:** Showcase your audience engagement metrics such as followers, reach, engagement rates, and demographics. Brands are often interested in partnering with influencers who have an engaged and relevant audience.

4.5.3 Research and Identify Potential Brand Partners:

- **UNDERSTAND THE BRAND'S target audience:** Research and analyze the target audience and brand values of potential partners. Ensure that their target audience aligns with yours and that their products or services are relevant to your audience.

- **Assess brand reputation and fit:** Evaluate the reputation, values, and credibility of the brands you are considering. Look for alignment between your values and theirs to maintain authenticity in your partnerships.

- **Consider brand history with influencers:** Research if the brand has a track record of working with influencers. Look for previous influencer collaborations and assess their success and authenticity.

4.5.4 Outreach and Collaboration:

- **CRAFT A COMPELLING pitch:** Tailor your outreach message to each brand, highlighting how you can provide value and meet their specific goals. Personalize the pitch to show that you have researched the brand and understand their needs.

- **Showcase your portfolio:** Create a portfolio or media kit that showcases your previous collaborations, audience insights, engagement rates, and the impact you've had on previous brand campaigns.

- **Collaborative ideas and proposals:** Propose specific collaboration ideas that align with the brand's goals and your strengths as an influencer. Offer creative suggestions for content formats, platforms, or campaigns that would resonate with your audience and promote the brand effectively.

4.5.5 Negotiate Terms and Compensation:

- **DETERMINE YOUR VALUE:** Assess the value you bring to the brand, including your audience size, engagement rates, content quality, and the reach of your platforms. This evaluation will help you negotiate fair compensation.

- **Consider different compensation models:** Negotiate compensation models such as flat fees, commission-based structures, product exchange, or a combination. Consider your audience's preferences and the campaign goals when deciding on the compensation model.

- **Contracts and legal considerations:** When finalizing partnerships, consider having a contract in place that outlines the scope of work, deliverables, timeline, compensation, and any exclusivity arrangements. Consult with legal professionals to ensure the contract protects your rights and interests.

4.5.6 Deliver Exceptional Campaigns:

- **ALIGN WITH BRAND GUIDELINES:** Adhere to the brand's guidelines and messaging while infusing your unique style and voice. Ensure that the content you create resonates with your audience while staying true to the brand's objectives.

- **Transparently disclose partnerships:** Clearly disclose your partnership with the brand in your content as per regulatory guidelines and platform policies. Use appropriate labels or hashtags such as "#ad," "#sponsored," or "in partnership with" to maintain transparency.

4.5.7 Nurture Long-Term Relationships:

- **PROVIDE POST-CAMPAIGN insights:** Share campaign performance data and insights with the brand after the collaboration.

Demonstrate the impact of your work and the value you brought to their campaign.

- **Maintain open communication:** Stay in touch with the brand and maintain a positive professional relationship. Engage in conversations, provide feedback, and explore future collaboration opportunities.

Conclusion:

DEVELOPING PARTNERSHIPS with brands as an influencer can open doors to exciting opportunities. Define your niche, create compelling content, research potential brand partners, craft personalized pitches, negotiate fair compensation, deliver exceptional campaigns, and nurture long-term relationships. By establishing successful brand partnerships, you can increase your visibility, monetize your influence, and provide valuable experiences for your audience. Remember to maintain authenticity and align with brands that genuinely resonate with your audience and align with your values.

CHAPTER CONCLUSION

AFFILIATE MARKETING and influencer strategies offer lucrative opportunities to earn income online by leveraging your online presence and audience. By understanding the basics of affiliate marketing, choosing profitable programs and products, building an engaged audience, promoting affiliate products on social media, and developing partnerships with brands as an influencer, you can monetize your online presence effectively. Remember to focus on providing value to your audience, maintaining transparency in your promotions, and continuously growing and nurturing your online community. With dedication, authenticity, and strategic collaborations, you can achieve success in affiliate marketing and influencer strategies.

Chapter 5: E-commerce and Online Selling

In this chapter, we will explore the world of e-commerce and online selling. We will discuss the steps involved in setting up an online store using popular platforms, sourcing and drop shipping products, effective product listing and optimization, digital product creation and selling, as well as managing inventory, shipping, and customer service.

5.1 Setting up an Online Store Using Popular Platforms:

SETTING UP AN ONLINE store is an essential step in establishing your e-commerce business. There are several popular platforms that can simplify the process and provide you with the necessary tools to create and manage your online store. Let's explore the steps involved:

5.1.1 Research and Choose an E-commerce Platform:

- **EVALUATE PLATFORM options:** Research popular e-commerce platforms such as Shopify, WooCommerce, BigCommerce, or Magento. Consider factors such as ease of use, customization options, available features, pricing plans, and scalability.

- **Assess your business needs:** Determine your specific requirements, including the number of roaducts you plan to sell, the level of customization you desire, and any specialized features you need (e.g., subscription services, digital downloads, or multilingual support).

- **Compare platform features:** Compare the features offered by different platforms, such as website templates, payment gateways, shipping integrations, inventory management, SEO tools, analytics, and customer support. Choose a platform that aligns with your needs and growth plans.

5.1.2 Sign up and Set Up Your Store:

- **SIGN UP FOR AN ACCOUNT:** Once you have chosen a platform, visit their website and sign up for an account. Provide the necessary information, including your store name, email address, and payment details.

- **Customize your store:** Follow the platform's setup wizard or onboarding process to customize your store. Choose a professional and visually appealing theme that reflects your brand identity. Customize your logo, colors, typography, and layout to create a cohesive and engaging online store.

- **Configure essential settings:** Set up payment gateways to accept customer payments. Configure shipping methods and rates based on your shipping preferences and locations. Define tax settings based on your business's legal requirements.

5.1.3 Add Products and Set up Categories:

- **CREATE PRODUCT LISTINGS:** Use the platform's interface to add your products one by one. Include essential details such as product name, description, price, SKU, and product variations (e.g., size or colour options). Upload high-quality product images that showcase your products effectively.

- **Organize products into categories:** Create categories or collections to group similar products together. This makes it easier for customers to navigate your store and find what they are looking for. Assign products to relevant categories to ensure a logical and intuitive store structure.

5.1.4 Set Up Payment and Shipping Options:

- **PAYMENT GATEWAYS:** Connect your preferred payment gateways, such as PayPal, Stripe, or Square, to your online store. Configure the settings to ensure smooth and secure payment processing for your customers.

- **Shipping methods:** Determine your shipping methods and rates. Set up shipping zones, define rates based on weight, dimensions, or destination, and integrate with shipping carriers like UPS, FedEx, or USPS. Provide accurate shipping information to customers during the checkout process.

5.1.5 Customize Store Policies and Legal Requirements:

- **PRIVACY POLICY AND terms of service:** Create clear and concise policies that outline how you collect, use, and protect customer data. Ensure compliance with privacy regulations, such as GDPR or CCPA. Include terms of service to establish rules for product returns, refunds, and customer interactions.

- **Legal requirements:** Familiarize yourself with local and international e-commerce regulations, including tax obligations, consumer rights, and data protection laws. Ensure your online store complies with these legal requirements.

5.1.6 Test and Launch Your Store:

- **TEST THE STORE FUNCTIONALITY:** Before launching your store, thoroughly test its functionality. Place test orders, verify payment and shipping integrations, and ensure that all pages, links, and forms work correctly. Conduct comprehensive testing to identify and resolve any issues or errors.

- Prepare for the launch: Set a launch date for your online store and create a marketing plan to promote its launch. Prepare promotional materials, social media campaigns, and email newsletters to drive traffic and generate initial sales.

- Launch and monitor: Make your store live and closely monitor its performance. Keep an eye on website analytics, track customer behaviour, and gather feedback to improve the user experience. Continuously optimize your store based on user data and market trends.

Conclusion:

SETTING UP AN ONLINE store using popular e-commerce platforms simplifies the process of establishing your e-commerce business. By researching and choosing the right platform, customizing your store, adding products, configuring payment and shipping options, and ensuring compliance with legal requirements, you can create a professional and customer-friendly online store. Remember to thoroughly test your store before launching, actively monitor its performance, and make necessary improvements to provide an exceptional online shopping experience for your customers.

5.2 Sourcing and Drop shipping Products

SOURCING PRODUCTS IS a critical aspect of running an e-commerce business. One popular method is drop shipping, which allows you to partner with suppliers who handle inventory storage and shipping. Here are the steps involved in sourcing and drop shipping products:

5.2.1 Determine Your Product Niche:

- **IDENTIFY A PROFITABLE niche:** Research different product categories and identify a niche that aligns with your interests, target audience, and market demand. Choose a niche that has room for growth and offers competitive opportunities.

5.2.2 Research and Identify Suppliers:

- **USE SUPPLIER DIRECTORIES:** Utilize online supplier directories like Alibaba, Oberlo, SaleHoo, or Worldwide Brands to find potential suppliers. These directories provide a list of suppliers in various industries, along with their contact information and product offerings.

- **Assess supplier credibility:** Evaluate potential suppliers based on their reputation, years in business, customer reviews, product quality, shipping options, and pricing. Look for suppliers with a proven track record of reliability and timely order fulfilment.

5.2.3 Contact and Establish Relationships with Suppliers:

- **REACH OUT TO POTENTIAL suppliers:** Contact the selected suppliers and introduce yourself as an e-commerce business owner interested in their products. Inquire about their terms, minimum order quantities (MOQs), pricing, shipping options, and any other relevant details.

- **Evaluate response and communication:** Pay attention to the supplier's responsiveness, willingness to provide information, and their ability to meet your requirements. Prompt and clear communication is essential for a successful partnership.

5.2.4 Negotiate Terms and Agreements:

- **DISCUSS PRICING AND terms:** Negotiate pricing, MOQs, payment terms, and any other terms relevant to your business. Seek competitive pricing that allows you to maintain profitability while offering competitive prices to your customers.

- **Request product samples:** Request product samples from potential suppliers to assess the quality, packaging, and overall customer experience. This helps ensure that the products meet your standards and align with your brand.

5.2.5 Set Up Drop shipping Arrangements:

- **FINALIZE AGREEMENTS:** Once you have selected a supplier, finalize the terms and conditions in a written agreement or contract. Clearly define the roles, responsibilities, and expectations of both parties.

- **Integrate with your e-commerce platform:** Set up integration between your chosen e-commerce platform and the supplier's systems. This allows for seamless order processing and automatic updates on inventory levels and order tracking.

- **Place customer orders:** When a customer places an order on your online store, forward the order details to the supplier, including the customer's shipping address and selected products. The supplier will then handle the packaging and shipping of the products directly to the customer.

5.2.6 Monitor and Manage Inventory:

- **REGULARLY COMMUNICATE with the supplier:** Maintain open lines of communication with the supplier to stay informed about inventory levels, new product releases, or any changes in pricing or shipping policies.

- **Monitor product availability:** Keep a close eye on product availability to avoid selling out-of-stock items. Coordinate with the supplier to replenish inventory in a timely manner and update your store accordingly.

- **Seek multiple suppliers:** Consider working with multiple suppliers to diversify your product offerings and reduce dependency on a single supplier. This can help mitigate risks and ensure a steady supply of products.

5.2.7 Provide Excellent Customer Service:

- **CUSTOMER INQUIRIES and support:** Be responsive to customer inquiries and provide timely support. Communicate with customers regarding order status, shipping updates, and any issues or concerns they may have.

- **Handle returns and refunds:** Establish a clear policy for returns and refunds and communicate it to customers. Coordinate with the supplier to manage returns and refunds efficiently.

Conclusion:

SOURCING AND DROP SHIPPING products offer a convenient and efficient way to manage inventory and order fulfilment in your e-commerce business. By conducting thorough research, identifying reputable suppliers, negotiating favourable terms, setting up drop shipping arrangements, monitoring inventory, and providing excellent customer service, you can build a successful business that offers a wide range of products to your customers. Continuously evaluate supplier performance and explore opportunities to expand your product offerings to stay competitive in the market.

5.3 Effective Product Listing and Optimization

CREATING COMPELLING and optimized product listings is crucial to attract potential customers and drive sales in your e-commerce business. Here are the steps to effectively list and optimize your products:

5.3.1 Craft Engaging Product Titles:

- **USE CLEAR AND DESCRIPTIVE titles:** Create product titles that accurately describe the product and include relevant keywords. Keep the titles concise and informative.

- **Highlight key features:** Include important product features or unique selling points in the title to grab the attention of potential customers.

5.3.2 Write Persuasive Product Descriptions:

- **FOCUS ON BENEFITS and solutions:** Clearly communicate the benefits of the product and how it solves a problem or fulfils a need for the customer. Explain how the product can improve their lives or address their pain points.

- **Use persuasive language:** Write compelling and persuasive product descriptions that engage and entice the reader. Use emotional language, storytelling, and customer testimonials when appropriate.

- **Include specifications and details:** Provide specific information about the product, such as dimensions, materials, colours, or any other relevant details that help customers make informed purchasing decisions.

5.3.3 Utilize High-Quality Product Images:

- **USE PROFESSIONAL PRODUCT photos:** Invest in high-quality product images that accurately represent the product and showcase its features. Use multiple images from different angles to give customers a comprehensive view of the product.

- **Ensure consistency:** Maintain a consistent style and background across your product images to create a cohesive and professional look. Use proper lighting and focus to enhance the visual appeal.

- **Enable zoom or 360-degree view:** Provide interactive features like zoom or 360-degree view options to allow customers to examine the product in detail.

5.3.4 Incorporate Search Engine Optimization (SEO) Techniques:

- **CONDUCT KEYWORD RESEARCH:** Identify relevant keywords and phrases that customers might use to search for products like yours. Use keyword research tools or Google's Keyword Planner to find popular and relevant keywords.

- **Optimize product descriptions and titles:** Incorporate targeted keywords naturally throughout your product descriptions and titles. Optimize meta tags, headings, and image alt text to enhance search engine visibility.

- **Utilize structured data:** Implement structured data markup, such as schema.org, to provide search engines with additional information about your products. This can improve the visibility and appearance of your listings in search engine results.

5.3.5 Provide Detailed Product Variations and Options:

- **INCLUDE PRODUCT VARIATIONS:** If your product comes in different sizes, colours, or other variations, clearly present these options to customers. Use dropdown menus or checkboxes to allow easy selection.

- **Specify pricing and availability:** Display pricing and availability information for each product variation to avoid confusion and provide a seamless shopping experience.

5.3.6 Incorporate Social Proof:

- **INCLUDE CUSTOMER REVIEWS and ratings:** Showcase customer reviews and ratings on your product listings to build trust and credibility. Positive reviews can influence potential customers' purchasing decisions.

- **Display trust badges and certifications:** If applicable, feature trust badges or certifications that validate the quality or authenticity of your products. This can instil confidence in customers and alleviate any concerns they may have.

5.3.7 Optimize for Mobile Devices:

- **ENSURE MOBILE RESPONSIVENESS:** Optimize your product listings and overall website design to be mobile-friendly. Test the responsiveness and loading speed of your product pages on various mobile devices to provide a seamless mobile experience.

5.3.8 Regularly Monitor and Update Listings:

- **TRACK PERFORMANCE metrics:** Use analytics tools to monitor the performance of your product listings, including click-through rates, conversion rates, and engagement metrics. Identify areas for improvement based on data insights.

- **A/B testing:** Conduct A/B testing on product titles, descriptions, or images to determine which variations lead to better engagement and conversions. Continuously optimize your listings based on the results.

Conclusion:

EFFECTIVE PRODUCT LISTING and optimization play a significant role in attracting and converting potential customers in your e-commerce business. By crafting engaging product titles, writing persuasive descriptions, utilizing high-quality images, incorporating SEO techniques, providing detailed variations and options, including social proof, optimizing for mobile devices, and regularly monitoring and updating your listings, you can improve the visibility, engagement, and conversion rates of your products. Continuously refine and optimize your listings based on customer feedback and market trends to stay competitive in the ever-evolving e-commerce landscape.

5.4 Digital Product Creation and Selling

CREATING AND SELLING digital products is a popular way to monetize your expertise and offer valuable content to your audience. Here are the steps involved in digital product creation and selling:

5.4.1 Identify Digital Product Opportunities:

- **ASSESS YOUR EXPERTISE:** Determine your areas of expertise, skills, or knowledge that can be packaged into a digital product. Consider your audience's needs, pain points, and interests to identify the type of digital product that would resonate with them.

- **Research market demand:** Conduct market research to understand the demand for digital products in your niche. Identify gaps or opportunities where your expertise can provide unique value to potential customers.

5.4.2 Choose the Type of Digital Product:

- **E-BOOKS AND GUIDES:** Create comprehensive written content in the form of e-books, guides, or manuals that provide valuable information, insights, or instructions.

- **Online courses:** Develop structured courses that teach specific skills or knowledge. Consider using platforms like Teachable, Thinkific, or Udemy to host and sell your courses.

- **Templates and resources:** Design and create templates, worksheets, checklists, or other resources that help your audience in their specific tasks or projects.

- **Software or digital tools:** Develop software applications, plugins, or digital tools that solve a particular problem or enhance productivity for your target audience.

- **Music, graphics, or digital art:** If you have creative talents, consider creating and selling digital music tracks, graphic designs, illustrations, or digital art pieces.

5.4.3 Plan and Create Your Digital Product:

- **OUTLINE YOUR CONTENT:** Create a detailed outline or curriculum for your digital product. Break it down into sections, chapters, or modules to provide a clear structure for your content.

- **Develop the content:** Write, record, or design the content for your digital product. Ensure that the content is well-organized, easy to understand, and provides value to your customers.

- **Consider multimedia elements:** Incorporate multimedia elements such as videos, audio recordings, images, or interactive elements to enhance the learning or user experience of your digital product.

5.4.4 Set Up a Delivery Platform:

- **CHOOSE A PLATFORM:** Select a suitable platform to host and deliver your digital products. Consider factors such as ease of use, security, payment integration, and customization options. Popular options include Gumroad, SendOwl, or self-hosting using plugins like Easy Digital Downloads for WordPress.

- **Set up product listings:** Create compelling product listings for your digital products. Include engaging descriptions, relevant images, and pricing information. Clearly communicate the benefits and value your customers will receive.

5.4.5 Establish Pricing and Payment Options:

- **DETERMINE PRICING:** Set a pricing strategy based on factors such as the value of your digital product, market competition, and customer preferences. Consider offering different pricing tiers or bundles to cater to a variety of customers.

- **Payment gateways:** Set up payment gateways that are convenient for your customers and integrate with your chosen platform. Popular options include PayPal, Stripe, or other online payment processors.

5.4.6 Market and Promote Your Digital Product:

- **DEVELOP A MARKETING plan:** Create a marketing strategy to promote your digital product. Utilize various channels such as your website, email marketing, social media, content marketing, and collaborations with influencers or affiliates.

- **Content marketing:** Create valuable content related to your digital product to attract and engage your target audience. Write blog posts, record podcasts, or create videos that showcase your expertise and provide a taste of what customers can expect from your digital product.

- **Build an email list:** Offer a free resource or opt-in incentive related to your digital product to encourage visitors to sign up for your email list. This allows you to nurture relationships, build trust, and promote your digital product directly to interested subscribers.

- **Leverage social media:** Utilize social media platforms to create awareness and generate interest in your digital product. Share sneak peeks, testimonials, or success stories related to your product. Engage with your audience and participate in relevant online communities.

- **Collaborations and partnerships:** Seek collaborations or partnerships with complementary brands, influencers, or experts in your niche. This can help expand your reach, tap into their audience, and gain credibility for your digital product.

5.4.7 Provide Customer Support and Updates:

- **CUSTOMER SUPPORT:** Set up systems to handle customer inquiries, provide technical support, or address any concerns related to your digital product. Promptly respond to customer queries and ensure a positive customer experience.

- **Updates and enhancements:** Continuously update and improve your digital product based on customer feedback or changes in your industry. Provide free updates or additional resources to existing customers to encourage customer loyalty.

Conclusion:

CREATING AND SELLING digital products allows you to monetize your expertise and provide valuable content to your audience. By identifying opportunities, choosing the right type of digital product, planning, and creating high-quality content, setting up a delivery platform, establishing pricing and payment options, marketing and promoting your product, and providing customer support, you can successfully sell your digital products online. Continuously refine and update your digital products to meet the changing needs and expectations of your customers, and leverage marketing strategies to reach a wider audience and maximize sales.

5.5 Managing Inventory, Shipping, and Customer Service

EFFICIENTLY MANAGING inventory, shipping, and providing excellent customer service are crucial aspects of running a successful e-commerce business. Here are the steps involved in effectively managing these areas:

5.5.1 Inventory Management:

- **UTILIZE INVENTORY management software:** Implement inventory management software or tools that help you track inventory levels, monitor product performance, and automate reordering processes. This ensures that you have adequate stock levels to fulfil customer orders.

- **Set up a centralized inventory system:** Maintain a centralized system that provides real-time visibility of your inventory across various sales channels. This helps prevent overselling, manage stock levels, and streamline order fulfilment processes.

- **Monitor product performance:** Regularly analyse sales data to identify popular products, slow-moving items, or seasonal trends. Adjust your inventory levels and marketing strategies accordingly to optimize sales and inventory turnover.

- **Establish safety stock levels:** Determine safety stock levels to ensure you have buffer stock to handle unexpected increases in demand or delays in restocking. This helps prevent stockouts and minimizes customer dissatisfaction.

5.5.2 Efficient Shipping and Fulfilment:

- **CHOOSE SHIPPING CARRIERS:** Evaluate shipping carriers such as UPS, FedEx, USPS, or regional couriers based on pricing, delivery speed, reliability, and coverage. Select carriers that best meet your customers' needs and align with your business requirements.

- **Automate shipping processes:** Integrate your e-commerce platform with shipping software or tools that streamline shipping processes. This allows you to generate shipping labels, print packing slips, track shipments, and provide customers with tracking information.

- **Optimize packaging and shipping methods:** Use appropriate packaging materials to ensure products are well-protected during transit. Optimize packaging sizes and weights to minimize shipping costs and avoid dimensional weight charges.

- **Offer shipping options and transparency:** Provide customers with various shipping options, such as standard, expedited, or international shipping. Clearly communicate shipping costs and estimated delivery times during the checkout process to manage customer expectations.

- **Manage returns and exchanges:** Establish a clear and customer-friendly return policy. Efficiently handle returns and exchanges by providing clear instructions, promptly processing refunds or replacements, and addressing customer inquiries or concerns.

5.5.3 Excellent Customer Service:

- **PROMPTLY RESPOND TO customer inquiries:** Aim to respond to customer inquiries, questions, or concerns within a reasonable timeframe. Provide multiple channels for customer support, such as email, live chat, or phone, to accommodate different customer preferences.

- **Personalize customer interactions:** Address customers by their names and provide personalized assistance whenever possible. Show empathy, actively listen to their concerns, and offer helpful solutions or alternatives.

- **Provide product information and guidance:** Be knowledgeable about your products and offer detailed information to customers. Help them make informed purchasing decisions by answering their questions, providing additional product details, or offering recommendations based on their needs.

- **Resolve issues and complaints professionally:** Handle customer complaints or issues promptly and professionally. Seek resolutions that are fair and satisfactory for both the customer and your business. Use negative feedback as an opportunity to improve and learn from customer experiences.

- **Collect and act on customer feedback:** Encourage customers to provide feedback on their purchasing experience. Actively collect and analyse customer feedback to identify areas for improvement and make necessary adjustments to enhance the customer experience.

5.5.4 Continuous Improvement and Optimization:

- **MONITOR CUSTOMER SATISFACTION:** Regularly assess customer satisfaction through surveys, reviews, or feedback platforms. Use this feedback to identify areas where you can improve your inventory management, shipping processes, or customer service.

- **Optimize operational processes:** Continuously review and optimize your inventory management, order fulfilment, and shipping processes to enhance efficiency, minimize errors, and reduce costs. Look for opportunities to automate or streamline repetitive tasks.

- **Keep up with industry trends:** Stay informed about industry trends, advancements in logistics or customer service technologies, and changes in customer preferences. Adapt your strategies accordingly to remain competitive and provide an exceptional customer experience.

Conclusion:

EFFECTIVE MANAGEMENT of inventory, shipping, and customer service is essential for a successful e-commerce business. By utilizing inventory management software, optimizing shipping processes, providing excellent customer service, and continuously improving your operations, you can ensure smooth order fulfilment, customer satisfaction, and business growth. Regularly monitor and analyse key metrics, adapt to changing customer needs, and strive for continuous improvement to deliver a seamless and exceptional experience for your customers.

CHAPTER CONCLUSION

E-COMMERCE AND ONLINE selling provide immense opportunities to reach a global customer base and generate revenue. By setting up an online store using popular platforms, sourcing products through direct methods or drop shipping, optimizing product listings, creating, and selling digital products, and effectively managing inventory, shipping, and customer service, you can establish a successful online selling business. Remember to continuously monitor and optimize your processes, adapt to market trends, and prioritize excellent customer experiences to thrive in the competitive e-commerce landscape.

Chapter 6: Passive Income Streams and Investing Online

In this chapter, we will delve into the world of passive income streams and online investing. We will explore various opportunities to generate passive income, such as dividend stocks, real estate crowdfunding, and peer-to-peer lending. Additionally, we will discuss how to create and sell digital assets, generate income through ad revenue and sponsored content, utilize robo-advisors and online investment platforms, and build a profitable blog or website with effective monetization strategies.

6.1 Passive Income Opportunities

PASSIVE INCOME REFERS to earning money with minimal ongoing effort or involvement once the initial work is done. In this section, we will explore various passive income opportunities that can help you generate income over time. Here are some popular passive income options:

6.1.1 Dividend Stocks:

DIVIDEND STOCKS ARE shares of companies that distribute a portion of their profits to shareholders in the form of dividends. By investing in dividend-paying stocks, you can earn passive income through regular dividend payments. Look for companies with a track record of consistent dividend payouts and consider reinvesting the dividends to compound your returns over time.

6.1.2 Real Estate Investments:

REAL ESTATE CAN BE an excellent source of passive income. You can invest in rental properties and earn income from monthly rent payments. Another option is real estate investment trusts (REITs), which allow you to invest in a portfolio of properties without the hassle of direct ownership. REITs distribute a significant portion of their taxable income as dividends to shareholders.

6.1.3 Peer-to-Peer Lending:

PEER-TO-PEER LENDING platforms connect borrowers with lenders, cutting out traditional financial institutions. By lending money to individuals or small businesses, you can earn interest income. Evaluate the risks associated with each loan and diversify your lending portfolio to minimize potential losses.

6.1.4 High-Yield Savings Accounts and Certificates of Deposit (CDs):

WHILE THE RETURNS MAY not be as high as other investment options, high-yield savings accounts and CDs offer a relatively low-risk way to earn passive income. These accounts provide interest on your savings or fixed interest rates over a specific period with CDs. Research financial institutions offering competitive rates to maximize your earnings.

6.1.5 Royalties from Intellectual Property:

IF YOU HAVE CREATIVE works such as books, music, patents, or trademarks, you can earn passive income through royalties. Licensing your intellectual property to companies or platforms can generate ongoing income whenever your work is used or sold.

6.1.6 Affiliate Marketing:

AFFILIATE MARKETING allows you to earn a commission by promoting other companies' products or services. You can join affiliate programs, share unique referral links, and earn a percentage of sales generated through your referrals. Choose products or services that align with your audience's interests and promote them through your website, blog, or social media platforms.

6.1.7 Digital Products and Online Courses:

CREATING AND SELLING digital products, such as e-books, online courses, software, or templates, can provide a passive income stream. Once you create and market these products, you can generate sales and income without continuous active involvement. Platforms like Udemy, Teachable, or self-hosting options can help you sell and distribute your digital products.

6.1.8 Automated Online Businesses:

BUILDING AN ONLINE business that operates on autopilot can be a great source of passive income. This could include drop shipping, affiliate marketing websites, or software-as-a-service (SaaS) platforms that generate income through subscriptions or advertising.

6.1.9 Renting Out Assets:

IF YOU OWN ASSETS LIKE a property, a car, or equipment, you can generate passive income by renting them out. Platforms like Airbnb, Turo, or peer-to-peer rental platforms allow you to earn income from your underutilized assets.

Conclusion:

PASSIVE INCOME OPPORTUNITIES offer the potential to earn money with minimal ongoing effort. Whether it's through dividend stocks, real estate investments, peer-to-peer lending, affiliate marketing, digital products, or other passive income streams, the key is to diversify your income sources, conduct thorough research, and continuously monitor and optimize your investments to maximize your earnings over time. Remember that passive income does require some initial effort and ongoing maintenance, but it can provide you with financial flexibility and the potential for long-term wealth accumulation.

6.2 Creating and Selling Digital Assets

CREATING AND SELLING digital assets can be a lucrative way to generate passive income. These assets can include a wide range of digital products, such as stock photos, graphics, templates, e-books, or online courses. In this section, we will explore the process of creating and selling digital assets. Here are the steps involved:

6.2.1 Identify Your Expertise and Niche:

DETERMINE YOUR AREAS of expertise and skills that can be transformed into valuable digital assets. Consider your passions, interests, and the needs of your target audience. Identifying a specific niche will help you create assets that cater to a focused audience.

6.2.2 Research Market Demand:

CONDUCT MARKET RESEARCH to identify the demand for digital assets in your chosen niche. Look for existing products or competitors to assess the competition and identify opportunities for differentiation. Determine the pricing range and quality standards for similar digital assets.

6.2.3 Choose the Type of Digital Asset:

BASED ON YOUR EXPERTISE and market research, decide on the type of digital asset you want to create and sell. Some popular options include:

- **Stock photos:** Capture high-quality photos of various subjects and themes that can be used by individuals or businesses for their marketing materials, websites, or social media.

- **Graphics and templates:** Create visually appealing graphics, design templates, website themes, or social media templates that can be customized and used by others.

- **E-books:** Write informative and engaging e-books on topics that align with your expertise and cater to the interests of your target audience.

- **Online courses:** Develop comprehensive online courses that teach specific skills or knowledge. Plan the course content, create video lessons, and design supporting materials like worksheets or quizzes.

- **Music or audio tracks:** Compose and produce original music or audio tracks that can be used for various purposes, such as background music for videos, podcasts, or multimedia projects.

6.2.4 Create High-Quality Content:

FOCUS ON CREATING HIGH-quality content that provides value to your target audience. Pay attention to detail, use professional tools and software, and strive for excellence in your creations. Ensure that your digital assets are visually appealing, well-organized, and easy to use or understand.

6.2.5 Set Up a Platform to Sell Your Digital Assets:

CHOOSE A PLATFORM OR marketplace to sell your digital assets. There are several options available, depending on the type of asset you're selling:

- **Stock photos and graphics:** Platforms like Shutterstock, Adobe Stock, or Etsy allow you to sell your digital images or graphic assets. Follow the platform's guidelines and upload your assets for sale.

- **E-books and online courses:** Consider platforms like Amazon Kindle Direct Publishing, Udemy, Teachable, or Gumroad to publish and sell your e-books or online courses. These platforms handle the distribution, sales, and payment processing for you.

- **Music or audio tracks:** Websites like AudioJungle or SoundCloud offer platforms to sell your original music or audio tracks. Upload your tracks, set the pricing, and reach potential customers interested in using your music.

6.2.6 Market and Promote Your Digital Assets:

EFFECTIVE MARKETING and promotion are crucial for attracting customers and generating sales. Consider the following strategies:

- **Build a website or blog:** Create a dedicated website or blog where you can showcase your digital assets, provide additional information, and establish your brand presence.

- **Content marketing:** Share valuable content related to your niche through blog posts, tutorials, or videos. This will help attract your target audience and establish your expertise in the field.

- **Social media marketing:** Utilize social media platforms to promote your digital assets. Share previews, behind-the-scenes content, or snippets to generate interest and drive traffic to your sales platform.

- **Email marketing:** Build an email list of potential customers and communicate regularly with them. Offer exclusive discounts, updates, or additional resources to encourage sales and maintain customer engagement.

6.2.7 Provide Customer Support and Updates:

ENSURE EXCELLENT CUSTOMER support by promptly addressing customer inquiries, providing assistance, or resolving any issues they may encounter. Regularly update your digital assets based on customer feedback, market trends, or technology advancements to enhance their value and relevance.

Conclusion:

CREATING AND SELLING digital assets can be a profitable venture, allowing you to generate passive income while leveraging your expertise and creativity. By identifying your niche, conducting market research, choosing the right type of digital asset, creating high-quality content, setting up a platform to sell your assets, marketing and promoting your products, and providing excellent customer support, you can successfully monetize your skills and knowledge. Continuously refine and expand your digital asset portfolio based on customer feedback and market demands to maximize your sales and passive income potential.

6.3 Generating Income through Ad Revenue and Sponsored Content

GENERATING INCOME THROUGH ad revenue and sponsored content is a popular way to monetize online platforms such as websites, blogs, or social media channels. In this section, we will explore how you can earn income through advertisements and sponsored content. Here are the key steps involved:

6.3.1 Build a Strong Online Presence:

ESTABLISH A STRONG online presence through a website, blog, or social media channels. Focus on creating valuable and engaging content that attracts a loyal audience. Consistently deliver high-quality content in your niche to build trust and credibility with your followers.

6.3.2 Ad Revenue through Display Advertising:

- **SIGN UP FOR AN AD network:** Join an ad network such as Google AdSense, media.net, or AdThrive. These networks connect publishers (you) with advertisers looking to display their ads on your platform.

- **Place ads strategically:** Strategically place the ad units on your website or blog to maximize visibility and click-through rates. Experiment with different ad formats, such as banners, text ads, or native ads, to find what works best for your audience.

- **Optimize ad performance:** Continuously monitor and optimize your ad placements and ad formats based on user engagement and earnings. Test different ad sizes, colours, or placements to improve click-through rates and overall ad revenue.

6.3.3 Sponsored Content:

- **DEFINE YOUR NICHE and target audience:** Clearly define your niche and target audience to attract relevant sponsors. Understand your audience's interests and needs to align with suitable brands for sponsored content collaborations.

- **Reach out to brands or join influencer networks:** Actively reach out to brands or join influencer networks that connect influencers with brands looking for collaborations. Create a compelling pitch that showcases the value you can offer to potential sponsors.

- **Negotiate terms and compensation:** Discuss and negotiate the terms of the collaboration, including the scope of work, content requirements, disclosure guidelines, and compensation. Consider factors such as the size of your audience, engagement rates, and the effort required to create the sponsored content.

- **Maintain transparency and authenticity:** When creating sponsored content, always disclose that it is sponsored to maintain transparency with your audience. Ensure that the sponsored content aligns with your brand and provides genuine value to your audience.

- **Track and measure performance:** Track the performance of your sponsored content campaigns, including metrics like engagement, reach, and conversions. Provide reports and analytics to sponsors to demonstrate the effectiveness of the collaboration.

6.3.4 Affiliate Marketing:

- **JOIN AFFILIATE PROGRAMS:** Sign up for affiliate programs relevant to your niche and audience. Many e-commerce websites, online marketplaces, or affiliate networks offer affiliate programs.

- **Promote affiliate products/services:** Recommend and promote affiliate products or services through your content, including blog posts, product reviews, or dedicated affiliate links on your website. Share your genuine experiences and provide valuable insights to drive conversions.

- **Track and optimize affiliate performance:** Use affiliate tracking tools or plugins to track the performance of your affiliate links and monitor conversions. Analyse which products or promotions perform best and optimize your affiliate marketing strategy accordingly.

6.3.5 Continuously Engage with Your Audience:

BUILDING A LOYAL AND engaged audience is crucial for long-term success. Continuously engage with your audience through comments, direct messages, or live interactions. Provide valuable content, respond to their queries, and foster a sense of community to maintain their support.

6.3.6 Stay Compliant with Regulations:

ADHERE TO RELEVANT advertising regulations and disclosure guidelines. Ensure transparency by clearly disclosing sponsored content and affiliate links, following guidelines provided by the Federal Trade Commission (FTC) or applicable regulatory bodies in your region.

Conclusion:

GENERATING INCOME THROUGH ad revenue and sponsored content requires building a strong online presence, creating valuable content, and establishing partnerships with relevant brands. By strategically placing display ads, joining ad networks, creating engaging sponsored content, incorporating affiliate marketing, and continuously engaging with your audience, you can monetize your online platform effectively. Always prioritize providing value to your audience and maintaining transparency to build trust and credibility. Regularly analyse your ad performance, sponsored content collaborations, and affiliate marketing efforts to optimize your strategies and maximize your earnings.

6.4 Utilizing Robo-Advisors and Online Investment Platforms

ROBO-ADVISORS AND ONLINE investment platforms offer convenient and accessible ways to invest and grow your wealth. These platforms use technology and algorithms to automate investment processes, making it easier for individuals to start investing and manage their portfolios. In this section, we will explore how you can utilize robo-advisors and online investment platforms. Here are the key steps involved:

6.4.1 Understand Robo-Advisors and Online Investment Platforms:

- **ROBO-ADVISORS:** Robo-advisors are online platforms that use algorithms to create and manage investment portfolios based on your financial goals, risk tolerance, and investment preferences. They typically offer a range of investment options, such as ETFs (Exchange-Traded Funds) or mutual funds.

- **Online investment platforms:** These platforms provide access to a wide range of investment options, including stocks, bonds, ETFs, or mutual funds. They offer tools and resources to help you research and select suitable investments based on your investment goals and risk tolerance.

6.4.2 Determine Your Financial Goals and Risk Tolerance:

- **IDENTIFY YOUR FINANCIAL goals:** Define your short-term and long-term financial goals, such as retirement planning, saving for a down payment, or funding a child's education. Your goals will help determine your investment strategy and time horizon.

- **Assess your risk tolerance:** Understand your risk tolerance, which refers to your willingness to accept investment fluctuations and potential losses. Consider factors such as your age, financial stability, and investment knowledge when assessing your risk tolerance.

6.4.3 Research Robo-Advisors and Online Investment Platforms:

- **COMPARE FEATURES AND services:** Research different robo-advisors and online investment platforms to compare their features, services, fees, investment options, and customer reviews. Consider factors such as account minimums, management fees, investment strategies, and available support channels.

- **Consider user experience:** Evaluate the user interface and ease of use of the platforms. Look for intuitive dashboards, helpful tools, educational resources, and portfolio tracking features that align with your preferences and investment needs.

6.4.4 Open an Account and Set Up Your Profile:

- **SIGN UP AND PROVIDE necessary information:** Open an account on your chosen robo-advisor or online investment platform. Provide the necessary personal and financial information required to set up your profile. This may include details about your income, employment, and investment experience.

- **Complete risk assessment questionnaires:** Many platforms will have risk assessment questionnaires to gauge your risk tolerance. Answer the questions honestly to help the platform determine an appropriate asset allocation for your portfolio.

6.4.5 Set Your Investment Strategy:

- **DEFINE YOUR INVESTMENT goals:** Specify your investment goals, such as capital appreciation, income generation, or a balanced approach. Communicate your goals and time horizon to the platform to guide the investment strategy.

- **Select your asset allocation:** Based on your risk tolerance and investment goals, the robo-advisor or online investment platform will recommend an asset allocation strategy. This determines the mix of stocks, bonds, and other assets in your portfolio. Review and adjust the recommended allocation if desired.

6.4.6 Fund Your Account and Automate Contributions:

- **FUND YOUR ACCOUNT:** Transfer funds to your investment account through bank transfers or other accepted methods. Some platforms may require a minimum initial deposit.

- **Automate contributions:** Set up automatic contributions to your investment account on a regular basis. This helps maintain a consistent investment habit and can be adjusted based on your financial situation.

6.4.7 Monitor and Rebalance Your Portfolio:

- **REGULARLY REVIEW YOUR portfolio:** Keep an eye on your portfolio performance and monitor the progress toward your investment goals. Use the tools and resources provided by the platform to track your investments.

- **Rebalance when necessary:** Over time, market fluctuations may cause your asset allocation to deviate from your target allocation. Rebalancing involves adjusting your portfolio to maintain the desired asset allocation. Many robo-advisors and online investment platforms automatically rebalance portfolios for you.

6.4.8 Stay Informed and Educated:

- **CONTINUE LEARNING:** Stay informed about market trends, economic news, and investment strategies. Many platforms offer educational resources, market insights, or newsletters to help you make informed investment decisions.

- **Seek professional advice if needed:** While robo-advisors and online investment platforms provide automated investment services, you may still require personalized financial advice. Consider consulting a financial advisor for more complex financial planning needs.

Conclusion:

ROBO-ADVISORS AND ONLINE investment platforms offer accessible and automated investment solutions for individuals looking to grow their wealth. By understanding your financial goals, risk tolerance, and conducting thorough research, you can choose a suitable platform. Open an account, set up your investment strategy, fund your account, and automate contributions. Regularly monitor your portfolio, rebalance when necessary, and stay informed about market trends. Utilize the educational resources and seek professional advice when needed. Utilizing robo-advisors and online investment platforms can help simplify the investment process and enable you to pursue your financial goals with confidence.

6.5 Building a Profitable Blog or Website with

Monetization Strategies

BUILDING A PROFITABLE blog or website involves creating valuable content, attracting a loyal audience, and implementing effective monetization strategies. In this section, we will explore the steps you can take to build a successful and profitable blog or website. Here are the key components:

6.5.1 Choose a Profitable Niche:

SELECT A SPECIFIC NICHE or topic for your blog or website that aligns with your interests and has the potential to attract a target audience. Research the market demand, competition, and monetization opportunities within your chosen niche.

6.5.2 Create Valuable and Engaging Content:

PRODUCE HIGH-QUALITY content that provides value to your audience. Focus on addressing their needs, answering their questions, or providing solutions to their problems. Use a mix of informative articles, tutorials, how-to guides, videos, or visual content to engage your readers.

6.5.3 Build a Professional Website:

SET UP A PROFESSIONAL website or blog using a content management system (CMS) like WordPress. Choose a visually appealing theme, ensure a responsive design that works well on all devices, and optimize your website for speed and user experience. Create clear and easy-to-navigate menus and categories to help visitors find the information they seek.

6.5.4 Drive Traffic to Your Website:

IMPLEMENT EFFECTIVE strategies to drive traffic to your blog or website. Some key tactics include:

- **Search engine optimization (SEO):** Optimize your content using relevant keywords, meta tags, and headers to improve search engine rankings and attract organic traffic.

- **Social media marketing:** Promote your content on social media platforms like Facebook, Twitter, Instagram, or LinkedIn. Engage with your audience, join relevant groups or communities, and share valuable content to attract visitors.

- **Guest blogging:** Contribute guest posts to other blogs or websites in your niche. This helps you establish your expertise, build backlinks to your site, and drive traffic from the guest blog's audience.

- **Email marketing:** Build an email list and send regular newsletters or updates to your subscribers. Offer exclusive content or incentives to encourage sign-ups and maintain engagement with your audience.

6.5.5 Implement Monetization Strategies:

TO GENERATE INCOME from your blog or website, consider the following monetization strategies:

- **Display advertising:** Sign up for ad networks like Google AdSense or media.net to display relevant ads on your website. Optimize ad placements and formats to maximize click-through rates and earnings.

- **Affiliate marketing:** Promote products or services through affiliate links. Earn a commission for each sale or action generated through your referrals. Join affiliate networks or directly partner with brands in your niche.

- **Sponsored content:** Collaborate with brands to create sponsored blog posts, reviews, or sponsored social media content. Disclose sponsored content transparently to maintain trust with your audience.

- **Digital products:** Create and sell digital products like e-books, online courses, templates, or software related to your niche. Use platforms like Udemy, Teachable, or self-hosted options to distribute and sell your digital products.

- **Consulting or services:** Offer consulting services, coaching, or freelance services based on your expertise. Use your blog or website to showcase your skills and attract clients.

6.5.6 Engage with Your Audience:

FOSTER A SENSE OF COMMUNITY and actively engage with your audience. Respond to comments, encourage discussions, and build relationships with your readers. Consider hosting webinars, Q&A sessions, or live events to connect directly with your audience.

6.5.7 Track and Optimize Performance:

REGULARLY ANALYSE YOUR website's performance and metrics. Monitor traffic sources, user engagement, conversion rates, and earnings. Use tools like Google Analytics or other website analytics platforms to gain insights into your audience's behaviour and preferences. Optimize your content, marketing strategies, and monetization methods based on the data collected.

6.5.8 Continuously Learn and Adapt:

STAY UPDATED WITH THE latest trends, industry news, and changes in your niche. Continuously educate yourself on new strategies, technologies, or platforms that can enhance your blog or website's performance. Adapt your content, marketing, and monetization strategies based on audience feedback and market demands.

Conclusion:

BUILDING A PROFITABLE blog or website requires dedication, consistent effort, and a strategic approach. Choose a profitable niche, create valuable content, drive traffic to your site, and implement effective monetization strategies. Engage with your audience, track performance metrics, and continuously learn and adapt to stay ahead. With perseverance and a focus on providing value to your readers, you can build a successful and profitable blog or website that generates income and helps you achieve your goals.

CHAPTER CONCLUSION

PASSIVE INCOME STREAMS and online investing provide opportunities to earn income and build wealth through various online platforms and strategies. By exploring passive income opportunities such as dividend stocks, real estate crowdfunding, and peer-to-peer lending, creating, and selling digital assets, generating income through ad revenue and sponsored content, utilizing robo-advisors and online investment platforms, and building a profitable blog or website with effective monetization strategies, you can establish multiple income streams and work towards achieving financial independence. Continuously educate yourself, adapt to market trends, and diversify your income sources to optimize your earnings and long-term financial success.

Chapter 7: Online Surveys, Microtasks, and Gig Economy

In this chapter, we will explore various ways to earn money through online surveys, microtasks, and gig economy platforms. These opportunities offer flexibility, quick income, and the ability to work from home or anywhere with an internet connection. We will discuss how to maximize your earnings through online surveys and market research, participate in microtasks and crowdsourcing platforms, explore gig economy platforms for quick and flexible work, and identify legitimate opportunities while avoiding scams. Let's dive into each section:

7.1 Maximizing Earnings through Online Surveys and Market Research:

ONLINE SURVEYS AND market research offer opportunities to earn money by providing feedback and opinions on various products, services, and market trends. To maximize your earnings in this field, consider the following strategies:

7.1.1 Research and Join Reputable Survey Platforms:

- LOOK FOR WELL-ESTABLISHED survey platforms with positive reviews and a track record of timely payments.

- Research the platform's reputation, user feedback, and rating on reliable review websites or forums.

- Join multiple platforms to access a wider range of survey opportunities and increase your earning potential.

7.1.2 Complete Profile Surveys:

- FILL OUT PROFILE SURVEYS honestly and thoroughly when signing up for survey platforms. These surveys help the platform match you with relevant surveys.

- Update your profile regularly to ensure that you receive surveys that align with your demographics and interests.

7.1.3 Actively Seek High-Paying Surveys:

- REGULARLY CHECK YOUR survey dashboard or email for new survey invitations. Promptly respond to surveys to increase your chances of qualifying.

- Prioritize surveys with higher payout rates or rewards. These surveys often require more time but can be more financially rewarding.

7.1.4 Participate in Focus Groups or Online Communities:

- SOME SURVEY PLATFORMS offer additional opportunities to participate in focus groups, product testing, or online communities.

- These activities often provide higher compensation and allow for more in-depth feedback and engagement.

7.1.5 Refer Friends and Family:

- TAKE ADVANTAGE OF referral programs offered by survey platforms. Refer friends and family to join the platform using your unique referral link.

- Earn additional rewards or bonuses when your referrals successfully complete surveys or reach certain milestones.

7.1.6 Be Consistent and Engaged:

- REGULARLY CHECK FOR new surveys and participate actively. Consistency increases your chances of receiving more invitations and qualifying for higher-paying surveys.

- Provide thoughtful and detailed responses in your surveys. Some surveys may have attention checks to ensure the quality of responses.

7.1.7 Cash Out Strategically:

- PAY ATTENTION TO THE payout options offered by survey platforms. Choose options that provide the best value for you, such as cash payments, gift cards, or other rewards that you can use.

- Consider redeeming your earnings once you reach a specific threshold to avoid any potential risks associated with keeping a large balance on the platform.

7.1.8 Explore Other Market Research Opportunities:

- LOOK FOR MARKET RESEARCH companies or agencies that offer additional opportunities beyond surveys. These may include participating in online panels, usability testing, or phone interviews.

- These activities often provide higher compensation and allow for more direct interaction with researchers.

7.1.9 Stay Active in the Survey Community:

- PARTICIPATE IN ONLINE forums or communities dedicated to sharing survey opportunities and experiences.

- Engage with other survey takers to learn about new platforms, tips for maximizing earnings, and potential survey scams to avoid.

Remember, *while online surveys can provide a supplementary income, they may not be a reliable source of full-time income. It's essential to set realistic expectations and consider other avenues for earning money online.*

Conclusion:

MAXIMIZING EARNINGS through online surveys and market research requires a strategic approach. Join reputable survey platforms, complete profile surveys, actively seek high-paying surveys, participate in additional research activities, refer friends and family, and cash out strategically. Consistency, engagement, and providing thoughtful responses will increase your chances of receiving more survey opportunities and maximizing your earnings. Stay active in the survey community to learn from others and keep up with new opportunities. With dedication and a proactive mindset, you can make the most of your online survey and market research endeavours.

7.2 Participating in Microtasks and Crowdsourcing Platforms

MICROTASKS AND CROWDSOURCING platforms offer opportunities to earn money by completing small, quick tasks or participating in larger projects. To make the most of your participation in these platforms, consider the following strategies:

7.2.1 Research and Choose Reputable Platforms:

- LOOK FOR WELL-ESTABLISHED microtask and crowdsourcing platforms with positive user reviews and a proven track record of timely payments.

- Research the platform's reputation, user feedback, and rating on reliable review websites or forums to ensure legitimacy.

7.2.2 Diversify Your Participation:

- JOIN MULTIPLE PLATFORMS to access a variety of microtasks and projects. Each platform may offer different types of tasks, allowing you to increase your earning potential.

- Explore different categories of tasks, such as data entry, transcription, content moderation, online research, or writing, based on your skills and preferences.

7.2.3 Develop Relevant Skills:

- IDENTIFY HIGH-DEMAND tasks or skills within the microtask ecosystem. Consider developing or enhancing your skills in areas such as translation, writing, graphic design, programming, or virtual assistance.

- Specializing in certain tasks can open up higher-paying opportunities and increase your chances of being selected for more lucrative projects.

7.2.4 Optimize Your Efficiency and Accuracy:

- FOCUS ON COMPLETING tasks efficiently without compromising quality. Time yourself to understand how long it takes to complete different types of tasks and optimize your workflow.

- Pay attention to instructions and guidelines provided for each task to ensure accuracy and avoid potential rejections or deductions.

7.2.5 Maintain a Good Reputation:

- BUILD A POSITIVE REPUTATION by consistently delivering high-quality work and meeting project requirements.

- Pay attention to user ratings and reviews that may be provided by clients or platform administrators. A good reputation can lead to more opportunities and better-paying tasks.

7.2.6 Explore Crowdsourcing Projects:

- SOME PLATFORMS OFFER larger crowdsourcing projects that require more time and involvement but offer higher compensation. These projects may involve tasks such as image categorization, data analysis, or content creation.

- Assess your availability and the complexity of the projects to determine if they align with your skills and interests.

7.2.7 Stay Updated with Platform Notifications:

- REGULARLY CHECK YOUR platform's notifications or email alerts for new tasks or project opportunities. Respond promptly to increase your chances of being selected for tasks with limited availability.

7.2.8 Be Mindful of Time and Effort versus Reward:

- EVALUATE THE TIME and effort required for each task in relation to the offered compensation. Prioritize tasks that provide a fair balance between time invested and the rewards received.

- Consider the potential for task automation or using productivity tools to optimize your workflow and increase your overall earning efficiency.

7.2.9 Seek Support and Community:

- PARTICIPATE IN ONLINE forums or communities dedicated to microtask and crowdsourcing platforms. Engage with fellow participants to learn tips, share experiences, and stay updated with platform changes or new opportunities.

Remember to set realistic expectations as microtasks and crowdsourcing may not always provide a steady or consistent income. It's advisable to explore other avenues for earning money online and diversify your sources of income.

Conclusion:

PARTICIPATING IN MICROTASKS and crowdsourcing platforms can be a convenient way to earn money online. By researching reputable platforms, diversifying your participation, developing relevant skills, optimizing your efficiency and accuracy, maintaining a good reputation, exploring crowdsourcing projects, staying updated with platform notifications, being mindful of time and effort versus reward, and seeking support and community, you can maximize your earning potential in this field. Keep in mind that building a consistent income through microtasks and crowdsourcing may require patience, adaptability, and a proactive approach.

7.3 Exploring Gig Economy Platforms for Quick and Flexible Work

GIG ECONOMY PLATFORMS provide opportunities for individuals to find quick and flexible work, often on a project basis. To make the most of these platforms and maximize your earning potential, consider the following strategies:

7.3.1 Identify Your Skills and Interests:

- ASSESS YOUR SKILLS, expertise, and interests to determine the types of gig economy platforms that align with your strengths. For example, if you enjoy driving, consider ride-sharing platforms, or if you have writing skills, explore freelance platforms.

7.3.2 Research and Choose Suitable Gig Economy Platforms:

- RESEARCH DIFFERENT gig economy platforms and consider factors such as reputation, user reviews, payment policies, and the availability of gigs in your area.

- Choose platforms that offer opportunities in your desired field or industry, as well as platforms that provide the flexibility and payment structure that align with your needs.

7.3.3 Optimize Your Profile and Portfolio:

- CREATE A COMPELLING profile or portfolio that highlights your skills, experience, and achievements. Include relevant samples of your work, certifications, or testimonials if applicable.

- Customize your profile to showcase your unique value proposition and stand out among other gig workers on the platform.

7.3.4 Set Competitive Pricing:

- DETERMINE COMPETITIVE pricing for your services based on market rates, your skill level, and the demand for your services in your area.

- Consider starting with competitive pricing to attract clients and build your reputation, and then adjust your rates as you gain more experience and positive feedback.

7.3.5 Respond Quickly to Gig Opportunities:

- ACTIVELY MONITOR GIG postings or notifications on the platform. Respond promptly to new opportunities to increase your chances of securing gigs before others.

- Make sure to read the gig requirements carefully and submit any necessary documentation or information promptly to avoid missing out on potential gigs.

7.3.6 Provide Excellent Service:

- DELIVER HIGH-QUALITY service and exceed client expectations to build a strong reputation and increase the likelihood of repeat business or referrals.

- Communicate clearly and promptly with clients and be responsive to their needs throughout the gig process.

7.3.7 Seek Reviews and Feedback:

- REQUEST FEEDBACK AND reviews from clients after completing gigs. Positive reviews and ratings can enhance your profile and attract more clients in the future.

- Use constructive feedback to improve your skills and performance, and continuously strive for excellence in your work.

7.3.8 Build Relationships and Networks:

- FOSTER POSITIVE RELATIONSHIPS with clients and fellow gig workers. Networking and referrals can lead to additional gig opportunities or collaborations.

- Engage with online communities or attend local events related to your gig work to expand your professional network.

7.3.9 Optimize Your Schedule and Availability:

- CUSTOMIZE YOUR AVAILABILITY settings on the platform to align with your preferred working hours or when demand for your services is highest.

- Be flexible with your schedule whenever possible to accommodate client needs and increase your chances of securing gigs.

7.3.10 Continuously Update Your Skills:

- STAY UPDATED WITH the latest trends and developments in your field to remain competitive in the gig economy.

- Invest time in learning new skills or enhancing existing ones to broaden your range of gig opportunities and potentially command higher rates.

7.3.11 Manage Your Finances:

- KEEP TRACK OF YOUR gig-related income and expenses for tax purposes. Consider using financial management tools or apps to streamline this process.

- Set aside a portion of your earnings for taxes and savings to ensure you are prepared for any financial obligations.

Conclusion:

EXPLORING GIG ECONOMY platforms can provide quick and flexible work opportunities. By identifying your skills and interests, researching suitable platforms, optimizing your profile, setting competitive pricing, responding promptly to gig opportunities, providing excellent service, seeking reviews and feedback, building relationships and networks, optimizing your schedule and availability, continuously updating your skills, and managing your finances, you can maximize your earning potential in the gig economy. Remember that success in the gig economy often relies on building a strong reputation, delivering high-quality work, and cultivating positive client relationships.

7.4 Identifying Legitimate Opportunities and Avoiding Scams

WHEN PARTICIPATING in online surveys, microtasks, and gig economy platforms, it's crucial to be vigilant and identify legitimate opportunities while avoiding potential scams. Here are some tips to help you navigate these platforms safely:

7.4.1 Research Platforms and Opportunities:

- BEFORE JOINING ANY platform, conduct thorough research to verify its legitimacy and reputation. Look for user reviews, ratings, and experiences shared by others who have used the platform.

- Be cautious of platforms that promise unrealistic earnings or require upfront fees to access opportunities. Legitimate platforms typically do not require payment from workers.

7.4.2 Trustworthy Payment Policies:

- LEGITIMATE PLATFORMS should have clear and transparent payment policies. Review the platform's payment methods, frequency, and minimum payout thresholds.

- Look for platforms that have a history of paying their workers on time and provide secure payment options.

7.4.3 Protect Personal Information:

- BE CAUTIOUS WHEN SHARING personal information online. Legitimate platforms should only ask for necessary information, such as your name, email address, or payment details.

- Avoid platforms that request sensitive information like your social security number or bank account password.

7.4.4 Beware of Red Flags:

- BE WARY OF PLATFORMS that make unrealistic promises or guarantees of high earnings with minimal effort. Remember that legitimate opportunities generally require time and effort to earn income.

- Exercise caution if a platform requests access to your personal social media accounts or asks you to download suspicious software or apps.

7.4.5 Verify Client or Employer Information:

- WHEN PARTICIPATING in microtasks or gig economy platforms, research the clients or employers offering the tasks or gigs. Look for information about their reputation, payment history, or any complaints against them.

- If possible, communicate directly with the client or employer through the platform's messaging system to establish credibility and clarify expectations.

7.4.6 Use Trusted and Verified Platforms:

- STICK TO WELL-KNOWN and reputable platforms that have been in operation for a significant period. Platforms with a large user base and positive reviews are generally more reliable.

- Research and join platforms that have a strong track record of providing legitimate opportunities and maintaining a safe working environment.

7.4.7 Read Terms and Conditions:

- FAMILIARIZE YOURSELF with the terms and conditions of the platforms you join. Pay attention to payment terms, dispute resolution procedures, and any clauses related to confidentiality or ownership of work.

7.4.8 Trust Your Instincts:

- IF AN OPPORTUNITY or platform seems too good to be true or raises suspicions, trust your instincts and exercise caution. Consult trusted sources, online communities, or professional networks for recommendations and advice.

7.4.9 Report Scams or Suspicious Activity:

- IF YOU ENCOUNTER A scam or suspicious activity on a platform, report it to the platform administrators immediately. This helps protect other users and maintains the integrity of the platform.

7.4.10 Stay Educated and Updated:

- STAY INFORMED ABOUT common scams and fraudulent practices prevalent in online earning platforms. Regularly educate yourself about the latest security measures, best practices, and tips for staying safe online.

Remember, due diligence and careful evaluation are essential when navigating online earning opportunities. By following these guidelines, you can identify legitimate opportunities, protect your personal information, and avoid falling victim to scams or fraudulent schemes.

Conclusion:

IDENTIFYING LEGITIMATE opportunities and avoiding scams is crucial when participating in online earning platforms. Conduct thorough research, trust reputable platforms, protect your personal information, be cautious of red flags, verify client or employer information, read terms and conditions, trust your instincts, report scams or suspicious activity, and stay educated and updated. By taking these precautions, you can safeguard yourself and make informed decisions while participating in online surveys, microtasks, and gig economy platforms.

CHAPTER CONCLUSION

ONLINE SURVEYS, MICROTASKS, and gig economy platforms offer opportunities to earn money in a flexible and convenient manner. By maximizing your earnings through online surveys and market research, participating in microtasks and crowdsourcing platforms, exploring gig economy platforms, and identifying legitimate opportunities while avoiding scams, you can tap into these avenues to supplement your income or create a full-fledged online earning source. Remember to research platforms, protect your personal information, and deliver high-quality work to establish a solid reputation and maximize your earning potential in these online earning fields.

Chapter 8: Scaling Your Online Business

Once you have established your online business and achieved initial success, the next step is to scale and grow your operations. In this chapter, we will explore strategies for scaling your online business, increasing profitability, building a remote team, leveraging automation and technology, expanding into new markets, diversifying income streams, and developing a long-term growth plan. Let's delve into each section:

8.1 Strategies for Scaling an Online Business and Increasing Profitability:

SCALING AN ONLINE BUSINESS requires strategic planning and implementation of effective strategies. Here are some key strategies to consider for scaling your online business and increasing profitability:

8.1.1 Analyse and Optimize Your Business Model:

- EVALUATE YOUR CURRENT business model and identify areas for improvement. Assess your products or services, target market, pricing, distribution channels, and competitive landscape.

- Identify opportunities for innovation or differentiation to stand out in the market. This may involve refining your value proposition, introducing new product features, or exploring new market segments.

8.1.2 Expand Your Marketing and Advertising Efforts:

- INCREASE YOUR MARKETING efforts to reach a larger audience and generate more leads. Utilize a mix of digital marketing channels, such as search engine optimization (SEO), pay-per-click

(PPC) advertising, social media marketing, content marketing, and email marketing.

- Develop a comprehensive marketing strategy that includes targeted campaigns, engaging content, and compelling offers to attract and retain customers.

- Use analytics and data tracking tools to measure the effectiveness of your marketing efforts and make data-driven decisions to optimize your campaigns.

8.1.3 Enhance Customer Experience and Retention:

- FOCUS ON PROVIDING exceptional customer experiences to build loyalty and increase customer retention. Pay attention to customer feedback, address their concerns promptly, and personalize your interactions.

- Implement customer relationship management (CRM) systems to track customer interactions, preferences, and purchase history. Use this data to personalize your marketing efforts and provide tailored recommendations to customers.

- Offer incentives such as loyalty programs, referral programs, or exclusive discounts to encourage repeat purchases and customer advocacy.

8.1.4 Streamline Operations and Improve Efficiency:

- IDENTIFY AREAS WHERE operational efficiency can be improved to reduce costs and increase productivity. Streamline processes, automate repetitive tasks, and leverage technology solutions to optimize operations.

- Invest in inventory management systems, supply chain optimization, and logistics to ensure smooth order fulfilment and minimize overhead costs.

- Utilize project management tools and communication platforms to enhance collaboration and efficiency among team members.

8.1.5 Explore Partnerships and Collaborations:

- FORM STRATEGIC PARTNERSHIPS with complementary businesses or influencers in your industry. Collaborate on joint marketing campaigns, cross-promotions, or co-creation of products or services to expand your reach and tap into new customer segments.

- Look for opportunities to collaborate with industry events, online communities, or thought leaders to increase your brand visibility and establish yourself as an authority in your niche.

8.1.6 Continuously Monitor and Adapt:

- REGULARLY MONITOR key performance indicators (KPIs) and analyse data to track your progress and identify areas for improvement. This includes metrics such as revenue growth, customer acquisition costs, conversion rates, and customer lifetime value.

- Stay updated on market trends, consumer preferences, and emerging technologies in your industry. Adapt your strategies accordingly to stay ahead of the competition and capitalize on new opportunities.

- Seek customer feedback and actively listen to their needs and preferences. Use their insights to refine your products or services and tailor your offerings to meet their evolving demands.

8.1.7 Invest in Talent and Skills Development:

- HIRE SKILLED PROFESSIONALS who can contribute to the growth and success of your business. Invest in ongoing training and development programs to enhance the skills of your team members.

- Foster a positive work culture and provide opportunities for career advancement to attract and retain top talent.

- Consider outsourcing or freelancing for specialized tasks or projects that can be efficiently handled by external professionals.

Conclusion:

IMPLEMENTING THESE strategies for scaling an online business and increasing profitability can help you achieve sustainable growth and maximize your business's potential. Regularly evaluate your progress, adapt to market changes, and prioritize delivering value to your customers. With careful planning, strategic execution, and a customer-centric approach, you can successfully scale your online business and achieve long-term profitability.

8.2 Building a Remote Team and Outsourcing Tasks:

BUILDING A REMOTE TEAM and outsourcing tasks can help you scale your online business by leveraging external expertise and resources. Here are some strategies to consider when building a remote team and outsourcing tasks:

8.2.1 Identify Tasks to Outsource:

- ASSESS YOUR WORKLOAD and identify tasks that can be outsourced. These may include administrative tasks, content creation, graphic design, customer support, social media management, or web development.

- Prioritize tasks that are time-consuming, repetitive, or require specialized skills that are not your core expertise.

8.2.2 Define Job Roles and Responsibilities:

- CLEARLY DEFINE THE job roles and responsibilities for each task or position you plan to outsource. This will help you identify the specific skills and qualifications needed for each role.

- Create detailed job descriptions that outline the tasks, deliverables, and desired outcomes for each role.

8.2.3 Find Qualified Professionals:

- UTILIZE FREELANCING platforms such as Upwork, Freelancer, or Fiverr to find qualified professionals for your outsourcing needs.

- Clearly communicate your requirements and expectations in your job postings, and carefully review candidates' profiles, portfolios, and feedback from previous clients.

8.2.4 Interview and Select Candidates:

- CONDUCT INTERVIEWS or video calls to assess the skills, experience, and cultural fit of potential candidates.

- Ask relevant questions to understand their expertise, working style, availability, and their understanding of your business objectives.

8.2.5 Establish Clear Communication Channels:

- SET UP EFFECTIVE COMMUNICATION channels with your remote team members to facilitate collaboration and efficient workflow.

- Use project management tools, such as Trello, Asana, or Basecamp, to assign tasks, track progress, and communicate project updates.

- Regularly schedule virtual meetings or video conferences to ensure effective communication and alignment with your business goals.

8.2.6 Provide Clear Instructions and Guidelines:

- PROVIDE CLEAR INSTRUCTIONS, guidelines, and deadlines for each task or project to ensure that remote team members understand the expectations and deliverables.

- Create standard operating procedures (SOPs) or training materials to provide step-by-step instructions for recurring tasks or processes.

8.2.7 Foster a Positive Remote Work Culture:

- NURTURE A POSITIVE work culture even with remote team members. Encourage open communication, provide regular feedback, and recognize their contributions.

- Foster a sense of teamwork and collaboration by organizing virtual team-building activities or encouraging informal communication channels, such as chat groups or virtual coffee breaks.

8.2.8 Ensure Data Security and Confidentiality:

- IMPLEMENT SECURE DATA management practices to protect sensitive information shared with remote team members.

- Utilize secure file-sharing platforms, password managers, and non-disclosure agreements (NDAs) to ensure data security and confidentiality.

8.2.9 Provide Ongoing Support and Feedback:

- REGULARLY CHECK IN with your remote team members to provide support, guidance, and feedback on their work.

- Encourage continuous learning and professional development by providing access to relevant resources or training opportunities.

8.2.10 Evaluate Performance and Adjust as Needed:

- SET PERFORMANCE METRICS and key performance indicators (KPIs) to evaluate the performance of your remote team members.

- Conduct periodic performance reviews and provide constructive feedback to help them improve their skills and performance.

Conclusion:

BUILDING A REMOTE TEAM and outsourcing tasks can help you leverage external expertise, increase efficiency, and scale your online business. By identifying tasks to outsource, defining job roles, finding qualified professionals, establishing clear communication channels, providing clear instructions, fostering a positive remote work culture, ensuring data security, providing ongoing support, and evaluating performance, you can effectively build and manage a remote team that contributes to the growth and success of your online business.

8.3 Leveraging Automation and Technology to Streamline Operations:

LEVERAGING AUTOMATION and technology can significantly streamline your online business operations, improve efficiency, and free up time for more strategic tasks. Here are some strategies to effectively leverage automation and technology:

8.3.1 Identify Repetitive and Time-consuming Tasks:

- IDENTIFY TASKS THAT are repetitive, manual, and time-consuming in your business operations. These tasks are prime candidates for automation.

- Examples include data entry, email marketing, inventory management, social media scheduling, customer support, and order processing.

8.3.2 Implement Workflow Automation:

- UTILIZE WORKFLOW AUTOMATION tools and software to automate repetitive tasks. For example, use tools like Zapier or IFTTT to connect different applications and automate data transfers or trigger actions based on specific events.

- Set up email autoresponders, drip campaigns, or chatbots to automate customer communication and support.

8.3.3 Use Customer Relationship Management (CRM) Systems:

- IMPLEMENT CRM SYSTEMS to manage customer interactions, track sales leads, and automate marketing campaigns.

- Use CRM features like lead nurturing, email automation, and sales pipeline management to streamline customer relationship management processes.

8.3.4 Streamline E-commerce Operations:

- UTILIZE E-COMMERCE platforms that offer automated inventory management, order processing, and shipping integration.

- Integrate your online store with payment gateways to automate payment processing and reduce manual intervention.

8.3.5 Employ Project Management and Collaboration Tools:

- UTILIZE PROJECT MANAGEMENT and collaboration tools like Trello, Asana, or Basecamp to streamline project coordination, task assignment, and progress tracking.

- Enable shared calendars, document collaboration, and communication tools to enhance team collaboration and eliminate inefficient manual processes.

8.3.6 Implement Data Analytics and Reporting:

- USE DATA ANALYTICS tools like Google Analytics or Adobe Analytics to track website performance, customer behaviour, and marketing campaign effectiveness.

- Generate automated reports and dashboards to monitor key performance indicators (KPIs) and make data-driven decisions.

8.3.7 Explore Artificial Intelligence (AI) and Machine Learning (ML) Applications:

- LEVERAGE AI AND ML technologies to automate tasks that require data analysis or decision-making. Examples include chatbots for customer support, recommendation engines for personalized product suggestions, or predictive analytics for demand forecasting.

8.3.8 Ensure Integration and Compatibility:

- ENSURE THAT THE AUTOMATION tools and software you choose can seamlessly integrate with your existing systems and processes.

- Evaluate compatibility with other tools, data formats, and platforms to ensure smooth operations and data flow.

8.3.9 Provide Training and Support:

- TRAIN YOUR TEAM MEMBERS on using automation tools effectively. Provide resources, tutorials, or workshops to help them maximize the benefits of automation.

- Offer ongoing support and troubleshooting assistance to address any issues that may arise.

8.3.10 Regularly Evaluate and Optimize:

- CONTINUOUSLY MONITOR the performance and effectiveness of your automated processes and technologies.

- Regularly review and optimize your automation workflows to ensure they align with your evolving business needs and goals.

Conclusion:

BY LEVERAGING AUTOMATION and technology, you can streamline your online business operations, improve efficiency, and reduce manual effort. Identify repetitive tasks, implement workflow automation, utilize CRM systems, streamline e-commerce operations, employ project management and collaboration tools, implement data analytics and reporting, explore AI and ML applications, ensure integration and compatibility, provide training, and support, and regularly evaluate and optimize your automated processes. With the right tools and strategic implementation, you can enhance productivity, scalability, and overall business performance.

8.4 Expanding into New Markets and Diversifying Income Streams:

EXPANDING INTO NEW markets and diversifying income streams can help your online business grow and increase its revenue potential. Here are some strategies to consider:

8.4.1 Conduct Market Research:

- IDENTIFY POTENTIAL new markets by conducting thorough market research. Consider factors such as market size, customer demographics, competition, cultural differences, and regulatory requirements.

- Explore both domestic and international markets to find opportunities for expansion.

8.4.2 Tailor Your Marketing and Offerings:

- CUSTOMIZE YOUR MARKETING strategies and offerings to cater to the specific needs and preferences of the target markets you are expanding into.

- Adapt your messaging, branding, and product features to resonate with the new market's cultural, linguistic, and social nuances.

8.4.3 Localize Your Content:

- TRANSLATE AND LOCALIZE your website, product descriptions, and marketing materials to effectively communicate with customers in the new markets.

- Consider hiring professional translators or localization experts to ensure accurate and culturally appropriate translations.

8.4.4 Develop Partnerships and Alliances:

- SEEK PARTNERSHIPS or collaborations with local businesses, influencers, or organizations in the new markets. They can provide valuable insights, access to a larger customer base, and enhance your brand's credibility.

- Explore joint marketing campaigns, cross-promotions, or co-branded initiatives to increase your visibility and reach in the new markets.

8.4.5 Expand Distribution Channels:

- EVALUATE AND ESTABLISH new distribution channels to reach customers in the new markets. This could include partnering with local retailers, distributors, or e-commerce platforms.

- Utilize online marketplaces specific to the new markets to increase your visibility and tap into their existing customer base.

8.4.6 Develop Localized Customer Support:

- PROVIDE LOCALIZED customer support to address the needs and concerns of customers in the new markets. This could involve hiring local customer support representatives or outsourcing customer service to multilingual professionals.

- Offer support channels in the local language, such as phone support, email, or live chat.

8.4.7 Introduce New Products or Services:

- CONSIDER INTRODUCING new products or services that cater to the needs and preferences of customers in the new markets.

- Adapt your offerings based on market demand and local trends. Conduct market research to identify gaps or opportunities for innovation.

8.4.8 Diversify Income Streams:

- EXPLORE ADDITIONAL sources of revenue to diversify your income streams. This can help mitigate risks and maximize your earning potential.

- Consider offering complementary products or services, creating digital products or courses, licensing your intellectual property, or generating income through affiliate marketing or advertising.

8.4.9 Embrace E-commerce and Global Shipping:

- DEVELOP AN EFFICIENT e-commerce infrastructure to facilitate sales and shipping to customers in different geographic regions.

- Optimize your website for international transactions and offer global shipping options to make your products accessible to customers worldwide.

8.4.10 Continuously Monitor and Evaluate:

- REGULARLY MONITOR the performance of your expansion efforts and income diversification strategies.

- Analyse key metrics, such as sales data, customer feedback, and market trends, to identify areas for improvement and make data-driven decisions.

Conclusion:

EXPANDING INTO NEW markets and diversifying income streams can unlock growth opportunities and increase revenue potential for your online business. Conduct thorough market research, tailor your marketing strategies, localize your content, develop partnerships, expand distribution channels, provide localized customer support, introduce new products or services, diversify income streams, embrace e-commerce, and continuously monitor and evaluate your efforts. By adopting a strategic and adaptable approach, you can successfully expand your reach, capture new market segments, and create a resilient and profitable business.

8.5 Developing a Long-Term Growth Plan:

DEVELOPING A LONG-TERM growth plan is essential for the sustained success of your online business. It provides a roadmap for achieving your business objectives and guides your decision-making process. Here are some steps to help you develop a robust long-term growth plan:

8.5.1 Define Your Vision and Goals:

- CLEARLY ARTICULATE your long-term vision for your online business. Identify what you want to achieve and what success looks like for you.

- Set specific and measurable goals that align with your vision. These goals could include revenue targets, market share expansion, customer acquisition, or geographic expansion.

8.5.2 Conduct a SWOT Analysis:

- PERFORM A COMPREHENSIVE analysis of your business's strengths, weaknesses, opportunities, and threats (SWOT).

- Identify your competitive advantages, areas for improvement, market trends, and potential challenges that may impact your growth strategy.

8.5.3 Identify Key Strategies:

- BASED ON YOUR SWOT analysis, develop key strategies to capitalize on your strengths, overcome weaknesses, leverage opportunities, and mitigate threats.

- Determine which areas of your business require strategic focus, such as marketing, product development, customer retention, or operational efficiency.

8.5.4 Break Down Your Strategies into Actionable Objectives:

- BREAK DOWN EACH STRATEGY into specific, actionable objectives. These objectives should be measurable and time bound.

- Assign responsibilities to team members or departments to ensure accountability and ownership for the objectives.

8.5.5 Develop Implementation Plans:

- CREATE DETAILED IMPLEMENTATION plans for each objective. Define the activities, timelines, and resources required to achieve them.

- Determine the key milestones and checkpoints to monitor progress and make necessary adjustments.

8.5.6 Allocate Resources:

- ASSESS YOUR RESOURCE requirements to execute your growth plan effectively. This includes financial resources, human capital, technology, and infrastructure.

- Allocate resources in alignment with your strategic priorities and consider any potential investments needed to support your growth objectives.

8.5.7 Monitor and Measure Progress:

- IMPLEMENT A SYSTEM to monitor and measure your progress towards your objectives. Define key performance indicators (KPIs) that align with your goals.

- Regularly review and analyse your performance data to identify areas of success and areas needing improvement.

- Use this information to make informed decisions, adjust strategies if needed, and optimize your business operations.

8.5.8 Continuously Learn and Adapt:

- STAY INFORMED ABOUT industry trends, technological advancements, and changes in the competitive landscape.

- Foster a culture of continuous learning and improvement within your organization. Encourage innovation, creativity, and experimentation to stay ahead of the curve.

- Seek feedback from customers, employees, and industry experts to gain insights and identify areas for improvement.

8.5.9 Review and Update Your Plan:

- REGULARLY REVIEW AND update your long-term growth plan to reflect changes in your business environment, market conditions, and internal capabilities.

- Set aside dedicated time to evaluate the effectiveness of your strategies and make necessary adjustments to stay aligned with your business goals.

8.5.10 Communicate and Align:

- ENSURE THAT YOUR GROWTH plan is communicated clearly across your organization. Align your team members' efforts with the long-term vision and goals.

- Encourage collaboration, cross-functional communication, and a shared sense of purpose to foster a cohesive and unified approach towards growth.

Conclusion:

DEVELOPING A LONG-TERM growth plan provides a roadmap for the sustained success of your online business. Define your vision and goals, conduct a SWOT analysis, identify key strategies, break them down into actionable objectives, develop implementation plans, allocate resources, monitor, and measure progress, continuously learn and adapt, review and update your plan, and communicate and align your team. By following these steps, you can navigate the ever-evolving business landscape, seize growth opportunities, and achieve long-term success.

CHAPTER CONCLUSION

SCALING YOUR ONLINE business requires careful planning, strategic execution, and continuous evaluation. By implementing strategies for increasing profitability, building a remote team, leveraging automation and technology, expanding into new markets, diversifying income streams, and developing a long-term growth plan, you can take your online business to new heights. Remember to monitor market trends, stay adaptable to changes, and prioritize delivering value to your customers. With a well-executed scaling strategy, you can achieve sustainable growth and maximize the potential of your online business.

A Heartfelt Thank You to Our Readers

Dear Readers,

We would like to express our sincere gratitude for choosing "Web Riches: The Roadmap to Online Earnings" as your guide to the world of online entrepreneurship. We understand that your time is valuable, and we are truly honoured that you have chosen to invest it in our book.

Our utmost appreciation goes to each and every one of you who embarks on this journey of digital wealth creation with us. Your commitment to learning, growing, and pursuing your dreams is inspiring.

We have poured our knowledge, experiences, and passion into this book, with the sole purpose of empowering you to achieve success in the online realm. It is our hope that the strategies, insights, and practical tips shared within these pages will propel you towards financial freedom and a life of abundance.

Thank you once again for joining us on this transformative adventure. Your support means the world to us.

Wishing you great success on your path to web riches!

Warm regards,

Avinash Walton

Don't miss out!

Visit the website below and you can sign up to receive emails whenever Avinash Walton publishes a new book. There's no charge and no obligation.

https://books2read.com/r/B-A-UQODB-QACWC

BOOKS2READ

Connecting independent readers to independent writers.

About the Author

Avinash Walton, whose birth name is Sonu Kumar Suman, is an Indian YouTuber, gamer, and podcaster. His mother is Rekha Devi and father is Brajnandan Prasad. He was born on 27th December 2003 in the Nawada district of Bihar, India. Avinash's journey from a small village to becoming a popular online personality is a testament to his determination, passion, and hard work.

Avinash's online presence is a testament to his versatility. He curates captivating content on his YouTube channels, each catering to different interests. Cut Facts Hindi is dedicated to sharing intriguing and educational facts, while BhaktYT showcases his gaming expertise and engages with the gaming community. Meanwhile, his podcast channel, Cut Facts, extends his reach to the realm of audio content.

With his dynamic skill set and creative pursuits, Avinash Walton has made a name for himself in the digital landscape. He continues to captivate and entertain his audience through his various online endeavors, leaving a lasting impression in the world of content creation.

Read more at https://linktr.ee/AvinashWalton.